What do I do about the kid who...?

50 Ways to Turn Teaching into Learning

Kathleen Gould Lundy

Pembroke Publishers Limited

Dedicated to Chuck Lundy and David Booth

© **2004 Pembroke Publishers**
538 Hood Road
Markham, Ontario, Canada L3R 3K9
www.pembrokepublishers.com

Distributed in the U.S. by Stenhouse Publishers
477 Congress Street
Portland, ME 04101
www.stenhouse.com

We acknowledge the financial support of the Government of Canada through the Book Publishing Industry Development Program (BPIDP) for our publishing activities.

We acknowledge the Government of Ontario through the Ontario Media Development Corporation's Ontario Book Initiative.

National Library of Canada Cataloguing in Publication

Lundy, Kathleen Gould
    What do I do about the kid who… ? : 50 ways to turn teaching into learning / Kathleen Gould Lundy.

Includes index.
ISBN 1-55138-165-6

    1. Teaching. 2. Motivation in education. 3. Underachievers. I. Title.

LB1025.3.L86 2004   371.3   C2003-907110-3

Editor: Kate Revington
Cover Design: John Zehethofer
Cover Photography: Photodisk
Typesetting: Jay Tee Graphics Ltd.

Printed and bound in Canada
9 8 7 6 5 4 3 2

Contents

Introduction: Thinking About the Students Who Keep You Awake at Night   *5*

    I See, I Wonder, I Hope   *5*

    Teaching "Hard" Skills in Soft Ways   *7*

    Finding Your Own Guiding Metaphors   *8*

    Helping Individual Students Find Their Voices   *9*

1. Establishing the Learning Environment   *11*

    A Viable Classroom Community   *11*

      1. Greeting and Checking In   *13*

      2. Setting Up a Login Centre   *14*

      3. Sharing Personal Goals and Needs   *16*

      4. Completing Personal Update Sheets   *17*

      5. Interviewing Your Students   *17*

      6. Playing Name Games   *19*

      7. Getting to Know Your Students Better   *21*

      8. Taking a Walk of Words   *22*

      9. Sharing Personal Stories   *24*

     10. Inviting "I am from..." Responses   *25*

2. Engaging the Students   *29*

    The Link Between Learning and Students' Lives   *30*

      1. Opening Up the Suitcase: Using Artifacts   *30*

      2. Reading Aloud to the Class   *32*

      3. Making and Working with Lists   *33*

      4. Step In/Step Back: Looking at Pictures   *34*

      5. Brainstorming Ideas   *36*

      6. Describing the Most Beautiful Thing You Know About   *37*

      7. Who Am I? Who Are You?: Teacher in Role   *38*

      8. Walk Around Reading   *39*

      9. Playing the Applause Connection   *40*

     10. Role-Playing Experts   *41*

3. Exploring the Curriculum   *43*

    What Helps Students Learn   *43*

      1. Cut to... : Creating Significant Images   *44*

      2. Step Out and Say Something   *47*

      3. Put Yourself on the Line   *47*

      4. Experimenting with Choral Speaking   *48*

      5. Working with Material Visually   *49*

      6. Working with Scripts   *50*

      7. Speaking in Role   *52*

8. A Bird's Eye View: I See, I Wonder, I Hope *53*
9. Getting Past the Words *53*
10. Saying It Through Movement *55*

4. Extending the Learning *57*

The Teacher's Role in Furthering Understandings *57*
1. Creating Questions to Deepen Understanding *58*
2. May There Be... *59*
3. Inner/Outer Circle *60*
4. A Corridor of Voices *61*
5. Interpreting Text in Readers Theatre *61*
6. Art Talks Back *63*
7. Moving in Response to Symbols *64*
8. The Shirt Off Their Backs *66*
9. Assuming a Dramatic Role *67*
10. Using Strategies That Lead to Log Writing *71*

5. Evaluating and Assessing the Learning *74*

Assessment as a Dynamic Process *74*
1. Keeping Anecdotal Records *75*
2. Interviewing to Prompt Reflection *76*
3. Using Exemplars to Establish Clear Criteria *79*
4. Developing Student Profiles *79*
5. Providing Rehearsal Opportunities *79*
6. Fostering Peer and Self Assessment *79*
7. Using Journals for Assessment *80*
8. Creating Rubrics *82*
9. Developing Portfolios *83*
10. Designing a Culminating Task *87*

Appendices *97*

Recommended Resources *105*

Professional Reading *107*

Index *110*

Acknowledgments *112*

Introduction:
Thinking About the Students Who Keep You Awake at Night

The bud
stands for all things,
even those things that don't
*   flower*
for everything flowers from
*   within, of self-blessing*

though sometimes it is
*   necessary*
to reteach a thing its loveliness,
to put a hand on the brow
of the flower
and retell it in words and in
*   touch*
it is lovely
until it flowers again from
*   within, of self-blessing*

By Galway Kinnell, from "Saint Francis and the Sow," in *Mortal Acts, Mortal Words*

What Do I Do About the Kid Who...? presents proven strategies to which teachers can apply their understanding, knowledge, intuition, experience, and skill, all to the end of creating classrooms where teaching works and learning matters. It is intended to help teachers establish viable communities of learning in their classrooms that address the needs of all students, including those with the potential to keep them awake at night.

We all know that one student's behavior can often influence the classroom dynamic. This book encourages teachers to ask questions about that student as they strive to establish and nurture classroom relationships, harness everyone's creativity, and set engaging contexts in which students speak, read, and write with real purpose. Often, the private questions that teachers ask themselves when they are alone in their cars, on the bus on the way home from school, or marking late into the night lead to further questions and discussion when they are asked in public settings, such as staff meetings and curriculum workshops. Usually, these once-private-now-public questions invite collective and involved critical thinking, group discussion, and interaction that lead to further research and rethinking of teaching practice.

In workshops, I often ask teachers to take a few minutes to think about the students who are on their minds a lot. Perhaps a student is disruptive in class or is unable to function in a group. Perhaps a student has just arrived in the class from another school or from another country or is so shy and quiet that she is often overlooked. Since the workshops I conduct often happen at the end of a long teaching day, teachers smile wanly as I ask them to focus in on that one student who is worrying them.

I See, I Wonder, I Hope

I ask workshop participants to imagine what these students are thinking and feeling as they enter the classroom. I then invite them to do some seeing, wondering, and hoping about the students. I ask them to write three phrases on a card and then to write about this student for ten minutes. On their cards, they write:

I see...
I wonder...
I hope...

Here is how one first-year teacher wrote about a boy in her Grade 8 classroom:

I see this boy coming into the classroom. He is always very boisterous and is intent on getting the attention of the other kids in the class. He never acknowledges me (even though I make a point of always saying "Good morning") and spends a lot of time making his presence felt. He is a lot taller and bigger than anyone else in the class and he seems to be larger than life. The whole classroom climate changes when he enters and there seems to be electricity in the air. I see him move to his desk. He often deliberately knocks over furniture and sweeps desks clean. I see his anger, his pain, his frustration, and his belligerence.

I wonder what makes him that way. Why does he feel that he has to have this kind of power? Is he self-conscious about his size? I wonder what he is like before he leaves his home to come to school. Does he have to prepare for this performance? Does he plan how he is going to enter the classroom? Is he aware of his behavior? Is he at all conscious about how much I want to support him? I also wonder what the rest of the kids really think of him and of me. Do they hope that I will do something to make him change? Do they wish that I gave my attention to them instead of to him?

I hope that I can connect to this student so that he can begin to relate to me and the others in a more respectful, more relaxed way. I hope that I can somehow make him trust me so that he does not have to put on this act. I am determined to reach out to him so that he can find ways to alter his behavior so that he can still be powerful, but in appropriate ways. I also hope to work with the class so that they can take some responsibility in all of this—so that we can all help him interact with the class in a more positive way.

Another more experienced teacher wrote about a student in this way:

I see a child who has come into the class at the end of March from another country. She is staying with relatives until her parents can get to Canada. Her facility in English is very limited. She has had a rough start. Not only has she come in the middle of the year, our class was away on an overnight field trip when she arrived and she had to sit in another class for the first few days in this school. She appears to be very shy. Even though I have tried to establish routines in my Grade 4 classroom, I am still struggling with many kids who crave attention and direction in their academic and social lives.

I wonder what this child is thinking and feeling. She seems to be in another world most of the time, alone. I often see her at recess walking by herself and even though I encourage the other children to play with her, she is often left out of things.

I hope that I can reach this student and help her feel more connected to the school and to the rest of the class. My students are so demanding that I often get home from school and realize that I have not connected to this child in any way during the day. I want to spend some time with her and to find out what I can so that she can get the support that she needs.

Even when I don't raise the issue of worrisome students, at the end of most classes or workshops, a few teachers always ask me, "But what do I do about the kid who…?" They then describe students who are often disruptive, silly, shy, attention seeking, worried about being wrong, too eager to please, dominating, or victimized by bullying. The list goes on. We then discuss these students, taking the opportunity to let our perceptions about them surface so that we can share ideas about teaching practice.

I am always moved by these discussions. Teachers have a strong desire to find ways of reaching these students by trying something new. They are intent on discovering new dimensions of themselves as teachers. As I interact with them, I am always reminded of what Ursula Franklin, in *The Real World of Technology*, says about the magic moment of teaching.

> Yet all of us who teach know that the magic moment when teaching turns into learning depends on the human setting and the quality and example of the teacher—on factors that relate to a general environment of growth rather than on any design factors set down externally. If there ever was a growth process, if there ever was a holistic process, a process that cannot be divided into rigid predetermined steps, it is education.

I hope that the ideas in this book will help teachers gain the confidence to spend time with the "teachable moment" and mine it for all it is worth as they find ways of connecting to *all* students, even those that appear to be on the outside of things.

Teaching "Hard" Skills in Soft Ways

I want to help young people know who and where they are, but I also want them to share what other people know, what work they do, what wonders people have already created in science, culture, and the arts. I want students to explore learning through doing but also through reflection and hard study. I want them to learn hard skills in soft ways. Most of all, I want my students, wherever I teach, to feel part of a compassionate learning community where they are honored as individuals, where they respect each other, and where they respect and love learning itself. In other words, I want it all.

Herbert Kohl

What Do I Do About the Kid Who…? is not about Special Education students, although many of the students with qualities described in the book may need extra attention and help. Herbert Kohl, in *The Discipline of Hope*, encourages teachers to teach "hard" skills in soft ways. Many of us who are involved in education—especially in the arts—are reluctant to describe any of the work that we do as "soft"; however, the ideas in this book offer teachers creative ways to engage *all* of their students in learning that is full of active exploration. The ideas will help students learn to make new knowledge their own.

What Do I Do About the Kid Who…? is intended to benefit students in many ways. I introduce resources that will help students feel that they belong in a classroom where they see themselves reflected back in the material chosen. I also describe activities intended to help students learn how to negotiate, listen, persuade, narrate, imagine, think deeply, argue for and against, make decisions, write for a variety of purposes, ask questions, pay attention to details, interpret body language, use their bodies to communicate, interpret texts, speak in role, give oral presentations, write for real purposes, and publish their writing for audiences that will read it. My focus is to make the day-to-day running of Junior/Intermediate classrooms easier and more organized, as well as more joyful and exciting, so that teaching and learning about and in language can happen in contextualized, respectful, and creative ways.

The suggestions made in *What Do I Do About the Kid Who…?* are based on five ways to organize classroom teaching:

- establishing meaningful contexts for teaching and learning
- engaging, or "hooking," students into wanting to know about what is being taught
- exploring material with students in active ways
- extending the experience so that the curriculum becomes more focused and reflective
- evaluating the learning that happens in classrooms

Each of these organizational structures is the focus of one of the book's five chapters which feature ten pertinent activities or strategies.

Finding Your Own Guiding Metaphors

All teachers want the students in their classrooms to feel that they are valued individually as well as collectively. They want their classrooms to be places where there is respect, not just tolerance; community, not just group process; relationships, not just connections; and empathy and compassion based on understanding, not just superficial encounters.

To help build this kind of community, I encourage teachers to find their own guiding metaphors. These can help teachers establish their visions for the work and relationships that will occur in their classrooms so that they can pursue teaching in a reflective way.

I encourage my student teachers to ask themselves, "What do I want my classroom to feel like, look like, sound like? What overriding quality do I want to establish from the beginning of the year to the end? *How will I get each one of my students to sparkle in his or her personal way?* How will I nurture, support, intrigue, and challenge them to take risks so that they will think critically about what they are learning and communicate their new knowledge to me and to others in exciting ways?"

In my work with pre-service teachers at York University, Faculty of Education, one of my student teachers, Jon Annis, envisioned his classroom like this:

At the heart of most Afro-Cuban rhythms is the clave pattern. A clave is a constant two-bar rhythmic pattern with specific positioning of the accents that repeat throughout a song. It is the foundation for Cuban rhythms and is the constant underpinning that any musician in the ensemble can hear if he or she becomes lost. The clave will be the foundation of my classrooms. It will represent the consistent strength of community inside the room. Its repeating pattern signifies what my students can expect every time they walk through the door. They will encounter a safe environment that guides them back on track when we get lost, one that holds us together while others catch up, and one that doesn't judge others on where they came from or where they are going. The clave is not always heard as musicians often feel its sensations even in its absence.

Emily Style and Peggy McIntosh, who work on the Seeking Educational Equity and Diversity Project at Wellesley College, see curriculum as an architectural structure that schools build around students. Style's metaphor of curriculum as window and mirror complements McIntosh's concern for multiple perspectives in education and embodies a view of school curriculum that provides students with opportunities to see not only the realities of others (curriculum as "window") but also the representations of their own realities (curriculum as "mirror"). If the student is understood as occupying a dwelling of self, education needs to enable students to look through window frames in order to see the realities of others and into mirrors in order to see their own realities reflected. When curriculum is viewed in this way, differences, as well as similarities, are validated, and students' understanding of themselves in relation to others is expanded.

Since 1994, I have developed a metaphor for my teaching that links with those of the window and mirror—a door. The door is a powerful image because of the nature and function of doors. Doors can be left ajar, opened wide, and shut while private discussion is held. In drama, we know that we can step through the door into other landscapes and see the world from different perspectives. Screen doors let in the light and the air and make us look at people, situations, and issues from a distance, screening out impurities so that we can see things clearer. Half doors let us hide some of the truth so that the other parts of a story can be illuminated. Doors with glass that fractures light help us see in prisms so that we are aware of the ambiguities of life and of multiple realities. Revolving doors help us come full circle in our understanding of the complexities and nuances of the human condition.

Sometimes, the doors of understanding won't budge and we, as teachers, need to be there to push them open. We need to have many strategies up our sleeves to illuminate thoughts and to transform hearts and minds. Sometimes, the door still jams and we have to find new ways to open it. Sometimes, there are locked doors and we have to decide how to find the key that will open the door safely to look on the other side.

Metaphors change as we think about teaching from different vantage points and teach different people in various contexts. At the moment, I hang on to the image of a "last"—an antique object that cobblers used to shape the leather so that they could fashion shoes. What I love about this object is its capacity to make me remember that if we stand in someone else's shoes for a while, we begin to understand what that person is thinking, feeling, imagining, learning, dreaming, hoping, and experiencing. Just as the cobbler makes shoes to enable life on the road to be more comfortable, safe, exciting, and bearable, I, as a teacher, must make the journey in the classroom all those things and more. I will work into the night to make sure that there are shoes for everyone. As I work, I remind myself that the time that students spend on the journey must be worth it in the end. I want the shoes that I create to be sturdy and of the best of materials so we can enter difficult terrain and never falter.

Helping Individual Students Find Their Voices

Although *What Do I Do About the Kid Who...?* focuses mainly on students in the Junior and Intermediate grades, the poem below, written by Erin B. Henry when she was seventeen, strikes a chord with many teachers. I often read "My Heart Is in My Throat" at the beginning or at the end of workshops and love the response I get. Teachers tell me that the poem reminds them of the tentativeness of learners, how difficult the passage from childhood to adulthood is

The delightful truth is that sometimes when we hear another out, glancing through the window of their humanity, we can see our own image reflected in the glass of their window. The window becomes a mirror! And it is the shared humanity of our conversation that most impresses us even as we attend to our different frames of reference.

Peggy McIntosh and Emily Style

for many of them, and how brave they have to be to meet the challenges both in and out of school.

Teachers usually ask me to read this poem to them again because the words help them remember that every one of their students needs to be given the time and the space to learn about new ideas, to ask questions, and to make their mark. Students also need opportunities to take risks and present their new learning in creative ways that clearly demonstrate the knowledge and skills that they have been mastering.

Teachers tell me that the poem, from a book titled *Things I Have to Tell You: Poems and Writing by Teenage Girls*, reinforces what they already know: that each student enters their classroom propelled by different needs, interests, learning styles, class backgrounds, values, cultures, languages, sexual orientation, racial identities, skills and intelligences. As they teach children how to become literate, thoughtful, and kind, they know that the diversity they encounter every day in their classrooms is both a gift and a challenge. They know that it takes time to help students learn to be comfortable and skilled at speaking in front of others, reading texts for meaning, writing responses that reflect their understanding, and getting along with one another day after day.

Finally, teachers tell me that they love this poem because it compels them to acknowledge that their calling is to help each student find his or her voice in the community called the classroom. Their goal is for everyone to sing their individual songs, laced with hopes and fears, with confidence, skill, knowledge, and joy.

Here is the poem. The response is yours.

My Heart Is in My Throat

Excuse me while I clear my throat—
I might pause with uncertainty
and turn a little red,
but please remain seated,
    I'll be with you soon.

Excuse me while I clear my throat—
you may hear a few squeaks and cracks,
and see me shake uncontrollably,
but please remain seated,
    I'll be with you soon.

Excuse me while I clear my throat—
I may close my eyes and look
invisible, but I am still here with you.
I have never done this before,
I have never sung a song
my song
of inner hopes and fears.
They may seem silly, childish, inscrutable
and may take me a minute, year
but please remain seated,
    I'll be with you soon.

CHAPTER 1

Establishing the Learning Environment

As a classroom community, our capacity to generate excitement is deeply affected by our interest in one another, in hearing one another's voices, in recognizing one another's presence.

bell hooks

bell hooks tells us that excitement in the classroom is generated through collective effort. In order to learn, kids need to feel safe. They also need to know that there is support for them intellectually, socially, physically, and emotionally. As they are challenged to take risks in their learning—to talk in class, to do science experiments, to read aloud, to write, to work in a group, and to explore dance, drama, music, and visual arts activities—they need to know that everyone in the class is rooting for them, that they are part of a community that respects and supports them. They will gain this confidence only if relationships that have already been established in the classroom are based on mutual respect.

At the beginning of the year, you need to spend time building relationships amongst your students so that positive things can happen in the classroom. This nurturing is not only your responsibility. Everyone needs to contribute to the building of a positive classroom community. Students need to be given opportunities to engage in activities that will let them get to know one another—not only on a superficial level, but in ways that make them think about others, empathize about their predicaments, and celebrate everyone's achievements.

As they learn about one another, students need to be made aware how their individual behavior affects everyone and what they can do, say, and change about their behavior to make the classroom dynamic work more effectively and coherently. This learning about character development is as important as academic achievement.

A Viable Classroom Community

A viable classroom community is based on clear expectations and a sound understanding of the students' knowledge and experiences of the world. It permits a kind of teaching called scaffolding, whereby teachers begin with a topic or concept near to students' experiences and build on their knowledge, development, and ability incrementally over a period of time. Scaffolding, a concept promoted by Lev Vygotsky, works when the environment is positive and encouraging, instructional support is intensive, concrete examples and visuals are used, and solving a meaningful, open-ended problem demands collective effort. Praise, warmth, and feedback are important in this interaction.

The value of student input

Everyone acknowledges that establishing rules, routines, and expectations in any classroom is important, but it needn't all be done by the teacher. Confident teachers ask for input from their students.

When I meet a class for the first time, I outline my expectations and then I negotiate solutions to problems that might be encountered as we try to set the goals and establish rules or routines. For instance, when I teach, I insist that no one talks while I am talking. I establish that rule on the very first day, but I spend time working with the students to see how we, as a class, can make this work. After I have outlined my rules, I ask for suggestions of how else we could make the classroom work to everyone's satisfaction. We talk about ways to decrease noise level, meet deadlines, do homework and hand it in, negotiate space, and solve conflicts.

Take negotiating space as an example. Junior and Intermediate students might like to have some input as to what kinds of information needs to be put on the walls and where certain information is better placed. Sight lines are also extremely important. Sometimes, students do not see or hear the material being presented due to where the teacher is standing or sitting. Some students need to face the teacher. Others need to have their own workspace. Many can handle working at a communal table.

Seating plans and space need to be flexible. At times, students need to sit in a circle so that they can see everyone. At other times, they need to be sitting at clusters of desks so that they can work cooperatively on a task. Many times, students will be working independently, doing silent reading, solving problems, or researching. They need to be able to work quietly away from the distractions of others.

Certain pieces of furniture or classroom areas may require special negotiation. If you have a sofa, how will this piece of comfy furniture be fairly used by all? Does there need to be a place in the room for social gatherings? Students should feel that this kind of thing is negotiable. Teachers can open up the discussion about the types of seating that all can live with and learn effectively in. If students feel that they have some sort of power in the negotiation they will be inclined to cooperate.

Positive feedback for the whole group

I find that giving genuine, positive feedback to the whole group works much better than singling out individuals who are doing things right or wrong. Instead of saying things like "I like how Ahmed is doing his work" or "I see Bridgett is sitting straight," I suggest another approach: one that is not competitive, that does not play off kids against one another and that does not cause envy or distrust. I look for positive moments and let the whole group know how I am responding to their behavior.

In one instance, I worked with a large group of inner-city elementary students of different ages at a leadership camp. The students were new to one another and initially felt uncomfortable. I stopped the group a few times. I told them how impressed I was by the risks they were taking. I acknowledged how difficult their work was and told them that I was pleased that they were being so generous despite that. Everyone began to relax and enjoy one another and the cooperative games they were playing. When everyone in a group is acknowledged and celebrated, the results are astonishing: everyone comes to work more effectively and efficiently with one another.

Appreciation of individual differences

The academic, artistic, and social work of the classroom is dependent on many things: what the student brings to the classroom in terms of background knowledge, experience, attitude, and learning style, and what the teacher models, expects, wants to happen, knows, values, and provides in terms of resources. So much of the work is dependent on the willingness of teachers to listen to their students, reflect back to them their cultures in the books and resources they choose, and find ways to celebrate the diversity in learning style, language, race, sexual orientation, gender, culture, and class background that they see before them.

To acknowledge and learn about diversity is a necessary part of curricular learning in the classroom. The work needs to be done if we are to empower students to understand the issues that have affected people in the past and help them find their voices to change their lives and the world around them in the future. It is important, therefore, to make our classrooms places where students experience equity as part of their daily lives, where they can be part of a community that affirms diversity and promotes equity. It is crucial for all of us to create learning environments that reflect our students' interests, racial and cultural backgrounds, family relationships, special needs and abilities.

Here is how we can address individual differences:

- First, we can find safe and honorable ways to become aware of the varied backgrounds and cultures of our students.
- Encouraged by Howard Gardner's research on different learning intelligences and Brian Cambourne's identification of conditions for learning, we can become aware of the learning styles of our students and teach as many of them in as many different ways as possible.
- We need to learn ways to foster inclusive behavior in our schools, behavior shown by both teachers and students.
- We can use teaching strategies and resources that will help us build communities of learning in our classrooms.

In many ways, *What Do I Do About the Kid Who...?* addresses these issues. Ten activities to establish the learning environment are presented in the balance of this chapter.

1. Greeting and Checking In

In the arts we know that beginnings and endings are very important parts of performances. I believe that the beginning of each day is crucial to the success of everything that happens after it. Time spent checking in with your students, giving an overall schedule for the day, outlining expectations and being open to

Questions to Ask Yourself

- How will the classroom be organized?
- Do I have the time, equipment, and materials needed?
- Is the material inclusive?
- What rules are necessary for safety and classroom management?
- Have I given my students some choice?
- Is there any mismatch between a student's language and the language of the school?
- Is there any mismatch between a student's experiences and the kinds of experiences presupposed by the teachers in the school?

negotiation from them can set a positive tone, take away anxiety, establish clear purpose, and allow for changes, interruptions, and the teachable moment.

Every new school year brings new relationships, configurations, and experiences. On the first day I always try to acknowledge everyone in a positive way so that every student feels significant. I can recommend a number of ways to greet and check in with as many students as possible. Before you begin your day, look over the class list and make sure that you read every name. Put a check mark beside the names of students who you would like to check in with at the beginning of the day. Consciously check off the names of students who are easy to overlook. I try to make time for them because I know that if I get to the ones who are usually overlooked, the payoff is great. They begin to feel noticed and are on your side when you try to establish routines and initiate new teaching and learning situations. I check in with the students whom I have identified right after the announcements. Checking in consists of making eye contact, saying good morning, and asking questions on an individual basis. Short conversations are usually the norm. This idea is based on research by Palincsar and Brown who were influenced by Lev Vygotsky's theories. The researchers looked at the insights that the teachers gain about their students' thinking processes as they talk to them about learning tasks and everyday events in the classroom.

I find that if I structure the classroom so that everyone has some time to get ready for the day ahead, then I can spend a few minutes with the students I have identified.

2. Setting Up a Login Centre

Sometimes, I feel that teachers are the most rushed people in the world. There is always so much to do, to be aware of, to document, and to teach! The day is filled with interruptions and changes to schedules. These can be disruptive to everyone unless there is some sort of structure to handle the incidents. I set up a Login centre in my classroom where students give me information and receive immediate feedback. I put a box with a slot in it at a central place in the classroom and I encourage students who have an important reason to talk to me to "login" so that I can deal with their questions or concerns. All notes from parents go into the Login centre and any information remains private unless I have the student's permission to talk to the class about the issue. (I have never used a lock, but you may if you wish.) The only stipulation is that I will look at information only if it is signed by the students. I do not respond to anonymous Login centre mail unless I have told the students to respond to something anonymously. I leave the sheets beside the box. I read the login mail as early in the day as I can and respond when appropriate or when my schedule allows. I always give my students a few minutes to organize themselves once they get into the class. They go to the Login centre if they need to make an appointment or write to me about their worries and concerns. I encourage them to do this and make sure that the students have sufficient time.

Page 15 provides an example of what a Login centre sheet might look like.

The Login Centre

Name: _____   Date: _____

Here is my question:

_____
_____

I am particularly worried about

_____
_____

I need to see you today because

_____
_____

   ❏ I can wait to see you tomorrow.
   ❏ Please do **not** share this with the class.
   ❏ You have my permission to address the class about this issue.

The Login Centre

Name: _____   Date: _____

Here is my question:

_____
_____

I am particularly worried about

_____
_____

I need to see you today because

_____
_____

   ❏ I can wait to see you tomorrow.
   ❏ Please do **not** share this with the class.
   ❏ You have my permission to address the class about this issue.

3. Sharing Personal Goals and Needs

After a few days of the new school year have passed, you can have students fill in sheets on personal goals and needs so that you will know a little more about them. They can work alone or in pairs. Ask them to respond to these prompts:

- I know that I am good at
- I want to get good at
- What I would like to contribute to the class:
- What I need from the school to achieve my goals:
- What I need from my classmates to achieve my goals:
- What I need from my teacher to achieve my goals:
- These situations in school make me worry that I am not going to be successful:
- These situations in school make me feel successful:
- When I feel that I am not going to be successful, I
- I dream of becoming

You can use the information obtained in a variety of ways. You can program for this kind of information, work hard to design groups that will have members that support one another, and work to find support for individuals who need help in reading and writing. Be sure to note changes in behavior. A reproducible sheet can be found as an appendix.

I know that I am good at
drawing

I want to get good at
reading and writing

What I would like to contribute to the class:
I know a lot about music and would like to have some time to tell the class about what I know.

What I need from the school to achieve my goals:
help in reading and writing
time and resources to do art

What I need from my classmates to achieve my goals:
quiet time away from the distractions of others

What I need from my teacher to achieve my goals:
extra time
more guidelines
understanding and patience
an opportunity to sketch my ideas first on paper so I will have a better chance of being able to write

These situations in school make me worry that I am not going to be successful:
working in groups where people dominate the discussion

> These situations in school make me feel successful:
> *when students in the class ask me to draw*
> *playing in the band*
> *some sports*
>
> When I feel that I am not going to be successful, I
> *tend to stop doing my homework and begin to become bored and silly in class. I*
> *don't pay attention and I talk to my friends*
>
> I dream of becoming
> *an artist, photographer or a manager of a music group*

4. Completing Personal Update Sheets

What do I do

about the kid who can't focus...who forgets bathing suits on swimming days, recorders on music days, money and permission slips on important deadline days?

I ask students who have trouble focusing to fill in sheets either in writing or with stickers to let me know how they are doing, what they would like to accomplish that day, what their worries are, and so on. If such a student runs into difficulty during the day, we then look at the sheet together and decide what the best strategy would be.

Page 18 provides an example of what this sheet might look like.

Most students do not deliberately forget things, but some seem to forget a lot. Part of growing up is learning to remember, and school should be a place where learning to remember is one thing that is taught and practised. Regretting the forgetting can play a big part in heightening the discouragement in classrooms. You and the class need to find strategies to minimalize these times. Be sure to work very carefully with the whole group at the beginning of the year.

You need to find ways to get kids to help one another and to help compensate for one another's lapses. Could there be a phone tree set up in the class so that everyone gets a call the morning of an event? Students who have a chronic memory problem will probably remember because they don't want to let their friends down, and if they are phoned just before they head out the door, they likely will remember. E-mail may be a good idea too *if* your students are hooked up and everyone agrees to check for messages. If a student is prone to forgetting his bathing suit, you could have some extras on hand. If a student keeps forgetting a permission slip and money is involved, you might begin to think that the cost of a trip is the issue. Inquire about that and if your suspicions are accurate, see if you can find a way for the school to help with the finances.

5. Interviewing Your Students

One of the ways that you can relate to your students is through interviews. I recommend meeting with your students three times a year (once per term) for twenty minutes in the library or in the classroom while other students work in groups. It's best to structure the interview so that it seems more like a conversation. Through interviews, I have found out amazing things about my students

Self-Regulated Learning

Personal goal for the day: _____

Here are some suggestions:

- ❏ to independently choose what I am going to read
- ❏ to listen to the read-aloud
- ❏ to begin the first draft of a writing assignment
- ❏ to listen to instructions
- ❏ to ask questions if I do not understand
- ❏ to move away from my friends if they are distracting me

- ❏ to read quietly
- ❏ to finish up my work
- ❏ to begin my research
- ❏ to find missing elements of my work
- ❏ to cooperate in the group
- ❏ to listen to everyone's ideas
- ❏ to contribute ideas to the group discussion
- ❏ Other: _____

What I can do for myself without help today:

- ❏ I can make a list of some ideas.
- ❏ I can go to the Book centre to find ideas to write about (characters, situations, problems, questions).
- ❏ I can find a partner and talk to him or her to get feedback.
- ❏ I can ask myself some questions and seek answers from a partner.

- ❏ I can begin to write and not worry about being right or wrong.
- ❏ I can have someone check my work.
- ❏ I can read my writing to someone and get feedback.
- ❏ Other: _____

What I need help with before I can begin:

- ❏ a place to write far from the distractions of my friends
- ❏ a fresh sheet of paper
- ❏ the list of requirements for the assignment

- ❏ a few minutes with the teacher to clarify some things
- ❏ a partner to work with
- ❏ Other: _____

Questions I have:

- ❏ When is the assignment due?
- ❏ How long does it have to be?
- ❏ Is there a rubric or assessment sheet?

- ❏ What should I do if _____ _____?
- ❏ Other: _____

What I am worried about:

- ❏ details
- ❏ expectations
- ❏ time

- ❏ problems in the group
- ❏ problems with resources
- ❏ Other: _____

and their feelings about school, me, the program, assignments, social interaction, themselves, and their relationship with friends in school. Sometimes, I would hear things that surprised and delighted me. At other times, I would discover things that disturbed me. Always, the interview afforded me the opportunity to connect with a student in a way that is impossible in a group or class setting. I spent the time listening carefully as I asked how things were going in terms of the program, the class relationships, and my actions as a teacher. I highly recommend this idea if you would be comfortable handling honest feedback and would be willing to change your program, make adjustments to your teaching strategies, re-explain, and rethink the structure of the groupings in your classroom to make learning more effective and inviting.

Here are some suggested questions to ask:

- How's it going?
- Have you managed to connect with most of the people in the class? What has made that easy? What has made that difficult? What kinds of things do you think we could do as a class to make us work together better?
- What do you enjoy about what we are doing in the class? Is there anything you dread doing? What could I do to make the experience better for you?
- What assignments have you enjoyed? What have been the challenges? How can I help you meet those challenges in the future?
- When it comes to school what do you worry about? Do you have any questions about the program that you would like to ask me? What are they?
- Do you think I have been clear about my expectations? What could I do to make things clearer?

6. Playing Name Games

Playing cooperative games can help students learn one another's names and connect with one another socially.

All these cooperative games can be played by the whole class as they stand or sit in a circle. They require students to establish eye contact with one another and provide an enjoyable way for students to learn one another's names and interact with laughter and fun. They can be played at the beginning of the year and again regularly.

Name and Motion: Ask the students to stand in a circle. Have them say their names one at a time and do an action. Have the rest of the class repeat the person's name and the action. Continue around the circle until everyone has had a turn. Tell the students that they do not have to plan the action. They should try to do it as spontaneously as possible. Play the Name and Motion game again, but in a number of different ways. Have the students say their names in an overly dramatic way, loudly, or in a whisper. Direct them to make actions that are squiggly, straight, or robot like. The rest of the class can mimic the name and motion.

Atom: Have students "walk to the empty spaces in the room" without bumping into one another. Tell them to walk quickly, change direction, walk on tiptoes, walk backwards, walk sideways, and so on. On a signal, such as a tambourine tap or a drum beat, have them freeze in time and motion. Congratulate them and then tell them to relax. Advise them that they are going to repeat the activity, but this time when you say, "Atom 3!" they are going to act as if they are atoms and join up with the students who are closest to them to form a group of three. They are to learn one another's names quickly. Then they are to walk throughout the room again. If you say, "Atom 5" they are to form a group of five. If anyone is left over, groups should hide those people in their constellations. It is very common to have leftover people. For example, if there are 21 students in the class and you say, "Atom 5," there will be four groups of five with one person left over. Go around and check to see the "extra" people hidden in the group. You might also make calls such as "Atom 2 + 3" or "Atom 7 − 2." Keep the groups moving and changing until everyone has been jumbled up and can name five people they couldn't name before.

Birthday Line: Have the students arrange themselves in two equal groups facing each other in a straight line. One line is Team X and the other is Team Y. Each team is to work together silently as quickly as members can. On your signal, have them arrange themselves in order of height, tallest people at one end and shortest people at the other. Then have the students arrange themselves in order of their birthday month. Have the students say when their birthdays are out loud and as they do, ask all of the students to pay attention. After this part of the game, ask the students if they heard any birthdays to which they can relate in some way. (My sister has the same birthday as Janet. Ahmed and I have the same birthday and we never even knew that last year!) Finally, have the students line up in alphabetical order based on first names. Ask them to say their names out loud so that everyone can hear the names and the way that they should be pronounced. (I play this game when I go into schools. It lets me hear how students want their names pronounced. I take special care not to mispronounce names and embarrass students.)

Back to Back/Face to Face: Have each student find a partner and tell partners to stand back to back just far enough away not to be touching each other. Have them change their position as you call out different commands such as "Face to Face," "Side to Side," "Shoulder to Shoulder," "Elbow to Elbow," or "Elbow to Shoulder." When you say "Change partners!" the students find another partner and the commands begin again. Students should be encouraged to find as many partners as possible and to learn their names in the split second of meeting!

The Seat on My Right Is Free: Have the students sit in a circle on chairs. Make sure that there is one empty chair. The person to the left of the chair says, "The seat on my right is free. I would like to invite (someone in the class) to sit beside me." The person who is invited crosses the circle, which frees up a chair. The game continues with the person to the left of the empty chair repeating "The seat on my right is free. I would like _____ to sit beside me." Make the rule that everyone should receive an invitation and that no person can be invited more than once.

Name Switch Now: Students stand in a circle. One person is It. It establishes eye contact with someone across the circle. It then says his or her name and the name of the person with whom eye contact was made. As It begins to walk towards this person, the person in focus establishes eye contact with another, says his or her own name and the name of the other, and begins walking towards that person. They switch places. The game should be played quickly and everyone should have a turn. Have students "give each other their eyes" as they say their names and somebody else's.

7. Getting to Know Your Students Better

The activities featured below provide opportunities not only for you to gain a better knowledge and understanding of your students, but for your students to come to know one another better in fun, engaging ways.

Heigh Ho: Have students sit in a circle. Appoint someone to be It. It stands in the middle of the circle and says, "Everyone who is wearing sandals, change places." Everyone has to move to another chair. It then runs to a chair and sits down. This will leave someone standing who then becomes It. The new It can say something else like "Everyone who watched TV last night, change places!" or "Everyone who wishes it was still summer vacation, change places!" If the person who is It says, "Heigh Ho" everyone must change places. Play the game quickly.

What Is My Wish?: Ask students to work in pairs. Have them decide who is A and who is B. The As tell the Bs three things about themselves, two of which must be factual. One of the things told must be a wish that A has. The wish should be shrouded in subtlety so that B has to listen actively and wonder which details are true and which detail is a wish. Here are some examples.

My name is Astrid. I was named after my mother's aunt who is a professional singer and lives in Los Angeles. I live with my cat, Abbie, a black and white cat that I found in the park where she had been abandoned. Which facts are true? What is my wish?

My name is Victor. I live in a house that has a wireless connection to the Internet. When I clap my hands, the lights in my bedroom go on or off. Which facts are true? What is my wish?

My name is Salvadore. I speak three languages fluently and have lived in five countries. It take me five minutes to walk to school because I live across the road. What is my wish?

My name is Saeeda. I love clothes and am lucky to know how to sew so I have new outfits every week. I have two cats and a brother. What is my wish?

After the students have guessed what are the facts and what are the wishes, let them spend some time talking to one another about their hopes and dreams. You can judge how much time is needed by being sensitive to the amount of discussion going on in the partner groups. You might decide to ask some students to introduce their partners to the class, or individuals can talk to the class about what they discussed with their partners.

May I Have Your Autograph?: Hand out copies of the Autograph Worksheet (page 23) to your students. Ask them to approach their classmates seeking answers to the questions on their sheets. Not only do they have to speak to a variety of people until they get yes answers, they need to establish details, such as where someone travelled outside the country or what great movie someone saw in the past four days. The autographs confirm that students shared personal data and may help students feel important. The completed forms can become the basis for class discussion and teacher review.

8. Taking a Walk of Words

When you begin a new theme or topic, you might want to find out what students think or know about it as a way in. If, for instance, you are looking at the themes of discrimination and prejudice, you might want to have them give you a personal response first. One of the ways that I do this is to place quotations around the classroom and ask students to take a "walk of words" and find the quote that connects to them in some way. Have them tell you why this quote is important to them.

Museum Walk of Words: Before they went to Michael Miller's play about Nelson Mandela, *In the Freedom of Dreams*, I worked with a Grade 5 class preparing them for what they were going to see and hear about the black leader. I taped quotes from the play as well as quotes from other champions of freedom, including Mandela, Mahatma Gandhi, Eleanor Roosevelt, and Mother Teresa, in strategic places in the classroom to make a Museum Walk of Words.

After recess, the teacher met with the class outside and told them they were going to take a Museum Walk of Words around the classroom to find the quote that meant the most to them. The students were told to enter the classroom silently, read all of the quotes posted on the walls, propped against the chalkboard, and pasted on the windows, and to stand beside the quote that resonated with them in some way. There were ten quotations. I played the theme music from *Schindler's List* and allowed the students some time to choose their quote. After they walked around the classroom, which took about five minutes, they ended up in groups or in pairs standing beside the words of their choice.

The groups sat together and talked to one another about their personal reasons for choosing these words. They then had a spokesperson summarize the discussion for the whole class. They created a still image as a group that represented their understanding of the quote and then read the quote out loud to the whole class.

Community Walk of Words: To extend this activity, the teacher asked the students to research ways that quotes by famous people have been memorialized and celebrated in buildings, paintings, signs, gravestones, memorials, walls, libraries, temples, synagogues, and churches. They went on a community walk in their neighborhood and found quotations on the buildings close to their school. In groups they researched the origin of those quotations and gave a presentation to another class in the school.

Autograph Worksheet

Find people in the room who have done at least one of the following things or have some of the qualities or attributes identified. Have them record their full name on the space beside the event, quality, or attribute. Ask them questions about the information. Record a short note on the sheet to remind yourself of the conversation. Make sure that you get as many names as possible on the sheet. Have people record their names only once. Try to meet as many people as possible! **Find someone who**

❏ has travelled outside the country this year (Autograph) _____

  Where? _____

❏ had something exciting happen to them today (Autograph)_____

  What happened? _____

❏ looks after their siblings after school sometimes (Autograph) _____

  Names of siblings: _____

❏ watched a great movie in the past four days (Autograph) _____

  Title: _____

❏ speaks more than one language fluently (Autograph) _____

  List: _____

❏ has a hobby (Autograph) _____

  What? _____

❏ has a favorite TV program (Autograph) _____

  Title: _____

❏ has a great book to recommend (Autograph) _____

  Title: _____ Author: _____

❏ has met someone famous (Autograph) _____

  Who? _____

❏ loves to cook (Autograph) _____

  Favorite food/recipe: _____

Creation of a Walk of Words: Picture books may provide beautiful quotations for students to consider. One class I worked with decided to use lines from the picture book *Prayer for the 21st Century*. The students placed their chosen lines on large mural paper in strategic places in the classroom. For instance, over the window they put

May those that live in the shadows be seen by those in the sun.

Near the entrance to the classroom, they placed

May the stars that gave ancient bearing be seen, still be understood.

As they left the classroom, they could look up and see

May the road be free for the journey; may it lead where it promised it would.

The Unveiling: An Illustrated Walk of Words: Another Grade 4 class collected their favorite quotes from the picture books that they were reading. They put up these quotes and illustrated mural paper with beautiful artwork.

On the door of the classroom, they made a large poster with the first part of the final words from Faith Ringold's book, *The Invisible Princess.*

We live in a peaceful village of freedom and love, in harmony with our brothers and sisters by all the stars above.

On the inside door of the classroom they wrote:

We live in a beautiful village full of happiness and joy, dedicated to the freedom of every man and woman and every girl and boy.

The making of the quotes became a visual arts project, and the class held a ceremony so that the various quotes could be unveiled. Parents, other students, and the administration were invited to this event and viewed all of the quotes on display. Each group of students gave a short presentation about why their quote was important to them. The groups also explained to the audience why they requested to have their quotes placed where they were.

9. Sharing Personal Stories

One of the ways to build relationships in the classroom is to have students engage in personal storytelling. They can do this in pairs, in small groups, or with the whole class. They can use these stories as "the textbooks of our lives." If we value what kids have to tell us we can then place the students' own experiences at the centre of the classroom.

Stories of Interdependence and Support: When working with the picture book *Barefoot*, I asked students to talk to a partner about who they relied upon to get them through their day. They each had a few minutes to talk to each other and relay this information. We then had a whole-class discussion about reliance—

You can't deny that students have experiences and you can't deny that these experiences are relevant to the learning process even though you might say that these experiences are limited, raw, unfruitful or whatever. Students have memories, families, religions, feelings, languages, and cultures that give them a distinctive voice. We can critically engage that experience and we can move beyond it. But we can't deny it.

Henry Giroux

how important it was for all of us to know that we can rely upon our family, friends, or community to be there for us when we need the support. It was a perfect discussion to have before we looked at the picture book, which is about how a runaway slave had to learn to rely upon the natural world to help him find his way to freedom.

Night Sky Imaginings: I remember working in a classroom with the picture book *The Orphan Boy* by Tololwa M. Mollel. As a way into the book I asked students to imagine that each of them was alone, lying in a field on a hot summer night. They were all experts in seeing and understanding the sky. They had watched it for many decades and had recorded their findings. They were very knowledgeable about the constellations and the different combinations and permutations of the night sky. On this particular night, as they watched, each one of them saw something that was out of the ordinary. They watched this phenomenon for a long time and realized that something was different and very strange. I played some music and let the room be silent for several minutes. Then I asked the students to share their imaginings with a partner. Later, we talked as a whole class. I had planned to go on and read the book, but the amount of storytelling and discussion about what people had really seen as well as what they had imagined was amazing. Many students had seen different things at different times in their lives. We carried on sharing our stories about the night sky until it was time for recess.

10. Inviting "I am from..." Responses

After I have spent a fair bit of time getting to know my class, I introduce a writing exercise that helps us relate to one another on a different level. I read about this exercise in Linda Christensen's *Reading, Writing, and Rising Up.*

"I am from..." is an excellent way to have students think about who they are and what made them that way. I ask them to examine what kinds of experiences, places, people, words, images, food, sayings, and readings have shaped who they are. They write about these things in a structured format and then share the writing with the rest of the class. When students listen to one another read their "I am from..." poems, something magical happens in the classroom.

Here is the basic structure of the activity, which you can modify to suit your students and their backgrounds and abilities. Hand out a sheet of paper to each student and say something like: "This exercise is going to help you write about who you are and what kinds of memories and things have shaped you. We are going to start in different ways and think about all sorts of things that take place in your lives. We will be roaming all over the place in our imaginations and in our memories, and you can record anything that you think you would like to share about yourself. We will have time to work with your writing and then you will have a chance to put it all together."

I have helped the students in a variety of ways. Sometimes, I do modelled writing with the class and write my own "I am from..." poem as a beginning. Other times, if the class needs less instruction and more time to think and imagine on their own, I give these directions: "Write the three words 'I am from' at the top of your sheet of paper. I want you to respond to the prompts I

What do I do
about the kid who is on the periphery of the classroom dynamic?

The ways that we organize classroom life should seek to make children feel significant and cared about—by the teacher and by each other. Unless students feel emotionally and physically safe, they won't share real thoughts and feelings. Discussions will be tinny and dishonest. We need to design activities where students learn to trust and care for each other. Classroom life should, to the greatest extent possible, prefigure the kind of democratic and just society we envision and thus contribute to building that society. Together students and teachers can create a "community of conscience" as educators Asa Hilliard and George Pine call it.

Linda Christensen

dictate to you. You can always change the items, but try to write down what first comes to mind."

These are the "I am from..." prompts that I usually provide:

- favorite thing to eat
- name of an interesting relative
- stores, parks or landmarks that you pass on your way to school
- family sayings (These can be written in your first language)
- an old toy or keepsake that you will never throw away
- the place that you keep that special item
- a place that you wish that you could return to when you have more time
- holiday food, songs, and traditions (*I am from green sprinkles on vanilla ice cream*)
- daily happenings (*I am from socks that will not stay up*)
- memories
- places where you feel safe and loved (*I am French mingled with English*)
- anything else that you would like to tell (*I am from school uniforms that were worn throughout the year; I am from the middle of the family*)

From there, students work in pairs.

"Read what you have just written to a partner. Have your partner read her poem to you. Discuss what you like about your poems. Ask questions about what some of the lines mean to you. Decide what you might delete, add, or repeat. Can you add lines that give us more information, but do not lose the impact?"

Initially, after I had come into the classroom to do the exercise, one Grade 6 student produced the poem below.

I am from a place where we speak many languages
I am from sadness and a hope for a better future
I am from peaceful evenings watching TV with my cousins
I am from cabbage soup, perogies and my grandmother's apricot nut cake

Then the teacher worked with the class further and the student, named Julia, sent me her revised version two weeks later.

I am from
A place where we speak many languages.
Sometimes we speak them all together in a mixing of voices.
I am from a sad number of days that I will always remember
Into a tomorrow of happiness yet to come.

I am from peaceful evenings watching TV with my cousins.
We sit on a comfy couch and try not to fight.
I am from cabbage soup, perogies and my grandmother's apricot cake.
I am from new beginnings—hellos, now, and no more good-byes.

This exercise works in many settings and in many ways. For example, one of my colleagues at York University, Marcela Duran, adapted it so that it became a reflective "We are from..." activity. At the end of the school year, the collective poems of small groups within a class full of student teachers, written early in

We Are From

we are from oceans of dancing
    passions
and islands of a thousand greens
from hollowness, from empty
    cupboards
we are sombre fragments floating

we are from the ashes of war
and the branches of peace

we are from the tune of our lips
and the beat of our hearts
from la pasta di nostra madre
from borum drums
from malt whiskey breath

we are snapshots, crêpes,
powdered sugar noses
we are from mango trees
and twilight church bells
from cantos de amor
and gold deserts of hope
from kilts and harlots
to flowing saris and veiled legacies

from Shabbat candles glowing
from the curved neck of a violin
from Easter eggs deep in drawers

we are from the cleanest dirt roads
    you've ever seen

Class poem edited by Aniko Szuks

the school year, were merged into one poem that meaningfully described the class as a community.

I have used this idea with reading material in all sorts of classrooms. In role, students have written character sketches using the "I am from..." exercise. For example, they have written as the runaway slave in *Barefoot*, as Killiken in *The Orphan Boy*, as Métis leader Louis Riel the night before he was hanged, and as the pigeon in *Wringer*.

Encouraging "Welcome Here" Responses: Sometimes, to help students feel "at home" in the classroom, you may choose to do additional activities to convey to students that they matter. You may have a kid come to the school in the middle of the year. By this time, routines and relationships are solidified, stories have been read and discussed, kids are in the middle of group assignments, and the class has shared many experiences and conversations. The newcomer may feel insecure, anxious, and very much on the outside of things.

Your class can think about this situation before it happens. As you are working with your students on building the relationships in the classroom, have them think about how they could welcome a student who may join the class at a later date. What if a new student does not speak English? What if the student is really shy? What if the student doesn't understand the rules that have been created? What accommodations can be made? As you ask your students these questions, you are encouraging them to think about others and to make that part of the way that they conduct their lives.

You might find that students come up with the best ideas about how to make a person feel welcome in the classroom. Here are some to get them started thinking. These suggestions are recommended for small groups.

- *A memory book group* is responsible for collecting and updating material about experiences that the class has had during the year. Members could work as archivists and watch out for material that could be put in the class memory book. They might include pictures, anecdotes, letters to guests who have worked in the classroom, pictures of other students who have arrived or left, and important moments so far. This memory book could be shared quietly with the newcomer after she or he has spent a few days in the classroom.
- *A curriculum folder group* is responsible for summarizing the learning that has happened in the classroom. The group should meet regularly to update the material and should keep the information in a folder, on a disc, or in some way that will be readily accessible to whoever needs to have a quick summary of what has been taught and learned. Students might include an overview of the work so far covered, big learnings to date, checklists of assignments, and an outline of work that lies ahead.
- *A welcoming group* has the responsibility of welcoming the student to the classroom and taking him or her on a tour of the school. It might be a good idea to include someone who has had the experience of coming to a school in the middle of the year. This student could inform the group about what kinds of things they might do to acknowledge the new student, to introduce the student to the class in a way that will make him or her feel welcome, and to lessen the stress of the new environment.

- *A survival kit group* prepares a survival kit, perhaps in consultation with someone who has had the experience of moving in the middle of the year. The group needs to think of what the newcomer will need the first day and get it ready. The survival kit could include such items as notebook and pen, map of the school, letter of welcome, facts to know about the class, teacher, and room setup, list of rules and regulations, and class list of names and pictures. The kit should not require much budget to develop.

It is crucial to make classrooms "places of possibility," as bell hooks calls them, where students and teachers have opportunities to negotiate rules, roles, relationships, and responsibilities and to be successful. The strategies described in this chapter are meant to help teachers and students establish classrooms based on mutual respect where exciting things can happen because people gain a positive sense of who they are and what they can achieve together. As *Open Minds to Equality* puts it:

To open [students'] minds and hearts to equality necessitates our building classrooms and school in which change is empowering, where work is meaningful and where community is genuine.... In such classroom and school communities differences are named and appreciated. It takes hard intellectual and emotional work on the part of teachers and students to struggle with the ideas and feelings that keep us apart. Yet we know that elementary and middle school students can understand difficult issues that relate to inequality, discrimination, power relations and social justice. They need adults to provide them safe space, language and opportunities to talk about their lives, struggles and visions.

CHAPTER 2

Engaging the Students

A young salesperson was disappointed. He had lost an important sale. In discussing the matter with the sales manager, the young man shrugged. "I guess," he said, " it just proves you can lead a horse to water, but you can't make him drink."

"Son," said the sales manager, "let me give you a piece of advice: Your job is not to make him drink. It's to make him thirsty."

From *Bits and Pieces*, January 14, 1999

All students come to school wanting to learn. They enter a world where they are stimulated by the presentation of new material, intrigued by the ideas that come out of discussions and activities with the teacher and their classmates, and have a personal interest in pursuing knowledge. Many of them, under the guidance of teachers, learn to read and write because they are presented with books and other interesting materials. They are taught reading and writing strategies that help them unlock meaning in the texts, they talk their way into understanding complex concepts by being encouraged to ask questions, they begin to think critically, and they are encouraged to present and represent these ideas in many different ways. Students who have been taught well feel a longing to know more and a confidence that they can independently and with their peers find out some of the answers to the multitude of questions that they have about living and learning in the world.

Sometimes, however, students become disengaged from school. Perhaps they do not connect to the material that is being presented and need to be "hooked" into it. They could be overwhelmed by what is being asked of them or perhaps they do not see the purpose of what they have been asked to do. They might be bored and frustrated by material that they do not relate to on a personal level.

How do we make school curriculum matter for all kids? How do we establish relevant, challenging, and open-ended contexts in classrooms where students are propelled into learning? How do we structure our classrooms so that students learn actively and critically assess and evaluate what is being presented to them? How do we introduce students to a myriad of ways of looking at the world? What strategies do we use to get them to the point where they are "thirsty" for more ideas and interaction?

Elliot Eisner tells us that curriculum should be concerned with the "invention of minds." Children are born with brains, he tells us, and it is up to us to develop these brains into minds. The everyday curriculum choices that teachers make are mind-altering devices. Curriculum is the total experience that the child has while he or she is connected to school. It encompasses what is taught, how it is taught, the resources available, guest artists, kinds of technology and its availability, field trips, extracurricular events, and homework support as well as the accommodations and modifications based on students' needs that are made in schools.

The Link Between Learning and Students' Lives

It is important to help students feel that there is a reason for them to learn what you are teaching. The challenge is to make the classroom a place where learning seems to be connected to their lives, issues, and events. Because the brain hungers for meaning, you have to spend time thinking about how to link the curriculum program to students' prior knowledge, understandings, and experiences. Just as I encourage my student teachers to do, ask yourself, "Why should this matter?" before you begin a teaching unit. Then you have to figure out how to "hook" the students into wanting to know more about the theme, topic, event, or novel. Ask yourself, "How will I present this material?" Will you bring in an old suitcase filled with artifacts that the students can unpack before you read the story? Will you go into role as someone from the historical era that you are studying and have them ask you questions? Will you encourage them to ask questions for information, to shape understanding, and to uncover new meanings? Will you play a game that will energize them? Will you introduce the concepts in the story by intrigue?

Think actively about these questions too: "How will I present the topic in such a way that they are fascinated and want to know more? Once they are 'hooked,' what will I do to hold their interest, build the momentum, and make them want to know more? How will I deepen the experience so that the students think critically and ask interesting questions? How will I encourage them to do authentic research to find out more? What interesting things will I get them to do or create with all of the information that they have discovered? How will I map backwards from a culminating task that is connected to all that they have learned in the unit?"

We often ask students to speak, write, and interact in group assignments without giving them a reason or a context to do the work other than the reward of marks. They have no stake in their learning. They are reluctant to do the work because it has no connection or meaning to them and they do not see the point. Often, those students who do the activities have learned at an early age to "play the game." They are successful in school not because they are any smarter than anyone else but because they have learned how to "do" school and go through the required hoops.

Teachers can foster real learning by making the curriculum personally relevant to their students. They have to find ways of hooking the students and then helping them make sense and meaning out of what they are learning. I spend time with teacher candidates helping them think of "ways in," or "hooks," to the lessons and units they teach. The hook must be authentic. It must be set up in such a way that students will be genuinely intrigued by an activity, question, image, artifact, anecdote, or story. They should want to know more about the material that is being taught.

Here are a number of "hooks" that I have developed over the years to get students interested in what is being introduced in the classroom.

Questions to Ask Yourself

- How will I catch the students' interest?
- How will I energize them for learning?
- How will I make them want to know more?

1. Opening Up the Suitcase: Using Artifacts

I use artifacts a lot in my teaching. I look for artifacts in antique stores, galleries, and other places, and I keep them in an old suitcase that also comes in handy in various teaching situations. I have a bunch of old keys, a number of colorful scarves, an assortment of old photographs, old maps, the collar of a dress, an antique puppet that is crumpled and disheveled, stones with symbols on them; a clown's make-up kit, a hat pin, an old perfume bottle, a collection of very old letters, and a diary written during the First World War. I use the artifacts in all sorts of different ways and I carefully design my lessons so that the artifacts are introduced at specific points to "hook" students into thinking about things. I use artifacts to introduce historical events, picture books, and new concepts, to engage student interest in a topic far from their experience, to help students make their way through difficult texts, to find common connections with their classmates, and to inspire discussion and debate.

Remembering Artifacts: Students love the fact that they are allowed to touch the materials, pass them around the circle in small groups, wonder about their use or origin, link them to the characters and incidents in the books and poetry they are reading, and use them in their oral presentations to the rest of the class. When I worked with a Grade 7 class that was preparing to re-create the trial of Métis leader Louis Riel, I asked the class to sit in a circle and then I brought in an old gingham tablecloth filled with these articles: the collar of an old dress, a noose, a baby's sock, an old letter, the beginning of a poem, a trial date notice, and headlines from a newspaper.

I took my time untying the string that held the articles together. I asked one student to hit a drum every time I took an artifact out of the collection and put it on a table in the middle of the circle. I asked that everyone remain silent. When the drum beats stopped, I covered the artifacts with the tablecloth and asked the students to record in their notebooks the items that I had put on the table. I told them that they would have an opportunity to handle each object in a minute, but they were to try to remember the seven items.

Using Artifacts to Tell a Story: We reviewed the list as a class and as we did so, I passed each object around the circle so that everyone could take a close look. I then asked them to get into groups and review the facts about Louis Riel's life and death. I asked them to write a list of the artifacts in the order that they would have appeared in the rebel leader's life. In other words, I wanted them to tell the story of Louis Riel's life and death through the artifacts alone. I then asked them to think of artifacts that they could substitute or add to Louis Riel's story. They could draw these or create them with art materials. The next day they shared the list of articles as well as the new ones that they felt were important to remember.

Predicting the Contents: Once, when I was invited to a school where they were celebrating National Book Week, I read *Dora's Box* to a Grade 3/4 class. I began the reading session by telling the students that I had found a box full of dangerous things that young children should be wary of. I put the box on my lap and asked them to tell me what they thought would be in it. The discussion was lively. Here was their list:

matches	car keys
sharp knives	bad Internet messages
indelible markers	

The teacher and I spent some time with them as they talked about why these items were dangerous and what rules their parents and guardians had put in place so that they would not be harmed.

I told them that I was going to read a book about a girl named Dora who lived a long time before there were cars, stop walks, and the Internet. I told them that I had put in the box things that she might be told to be careful of. I opened the box and took out a hat pin with a very sharp point. (They had never heard of a hat pin but I brought along an old hat and showed them how it worked!), a candle, and a prickly rose thorn.

We talked about why these items might be dangerous and compared them to the list that we had created earlier. I asked them if they thought that there were more things to be careful about now than in the past. Then I read *Dora's Box*, the story of an overprotected child who finds out that she needs to be aware of the dangers of the world in order to understand them and to be more sensitive about how they affect people.

2. Reading Aloud to the Class

Another way to engage the class is to read aloud. The time is well spent and renders positive results. Reading aloud creates a bond amongst the student listeners because they experience something together. It often causes significant changes in students' attitudes towards reading too. That is because it allows them to

- create images in their minds
- hear and see models of proficient reading
- listen to "good" writing
- build content-area background knowledge
- find pleasure in the listening experience
- hear language that they would not otherwise be aware of
- anticipate what will happen next and hone their skills of prediction
- fall in love with language

Janet Allen sums up the benefits of reading aloud for students in her book, *Yellow Brick Roads: Shared and Guided Paths to Independent Reading (4–12)*. She tells teachers to find texts that are filled with "charm, magic, impact and appeal." (p. 48) "Sometimes, I think, we become aware of how far struggling readers are behind their peers and we attempt to make up for those differences by jumping into programs heavily weighted toward strategies and skills. While many of the skills and strategies are necessary for successful reading and writing, it is interest and motivation that have to be fostered before students can realize there is anything worth reading."

Great Beginnings: Sometimes, students find it difficult to begin a book so I read aloud a selection of first chapters to entice them into reading. For example, I might read the opening chapters of these Junior and Intermediate novels: *Wringer*, *Silent to the Bone*, *The True Confessions of Charlotte Doyle*, *Fat Chance*, and *Hatchet*.

I am often invited into schools to inspire students to read. I like to bring in novels that will draw kids into the story and make them want to read the books themselves. Here are some titles that you might introduce students to through reading aloud:

Junior Level
- *The Summer of the Swans*, by Betsy Byers
- *I Know What You Did Last Summer*, by Lois Duncan
- *Tuck Everlasting*, by Natalie Babbitt
- *Underground to Canada*, by Barbara Smucker
- *The Sky Is Falling*, by Kit Pearson
- *Silverwing*, by Kenneth Oppel
- *Sunwing*, by Kenneth Oppel

Intermediate Level
- *Nothing but the Truth*, by Avi
- *Angel Square*, by Brian Doyle
- *Paradise Café and Other Stories*, by Martha Brooks
- *Silent to the Bone*, by E.L. Konigsburg
- *The Burning Time*, by Carol Matas
- *Slake's Limbo*, by Felice Holman
- *The Root Cellar*, by Janet Lunn

Reading from Overhead Transparencies: You can find ways to read student writing which will also bring great pleasure to the classroom experience. You might project student writing on an overhead transparency and read it aloud so that students can see their work come alive through your voice.

3. Making and Working with Lists

I often begin a class by asking the students to write a list. I tell them that they will understand more as we work and they are happy to wonder as I dictate the list to them. When one of my student teachers tried this idea, she heard a Grade 5 student saying, "This is so exciting." The student didn't even know what was going to happen next.

I provide each student with an index card for the writing. I use a lot of index cards when I teach because there is something about index cards that frees students up. A big piece of paper makes those students who worry about writing even more anxious about the length of the writing that may be required.

Determining a Short List: Once, when I worked with a Grade 4 class on the short story "The Choice," by Wayland Young, I asked them to write down a list of twenty items: change of clothes, statistics on various countries, first aid kit, weapon, shampoo, oxygen mask, diary or logbook, personal computer, newspaper, matches, compass, diamonds and gold, watch, food and water, tape recorder, camera, personal identification, history book, map of the world, and pocket mirror. I then invited them to work independently and decide on the four items they considered essential if they were to travel into the future. I did not provide more details. Next, students worked with partners discussing their choices and comparing items. They were allowed to change their minds. Each duo then connected with two other partner groups, creating a group of six where members were expected to listen to one another with open minds and

What do I do
*about the kid who feels
daunted by writing?*

reach a consensus on the five or six most essential items. Each group chose a spokesperson to report to the class.

Working with a list in this way has another benefit. In every class there are those who tend to dominate discussion and those who are silent, though engaged. I have found that one of the best ways to get kids to work cooperatively is to make sure that they have had time to think about the work that they have been asked to do: first, as an individual; then, with a partner; and then, in a small group. Students tend to find their public voices in stages rather than by being put on the spot right at the beginning. I also ask students to be mindful of their partners and other group members so that everyone is able to contribute ideas and be heard. The intent is to counterbalance the tendencies of some students to dominate group work and thereby prevent others from getting discouraged and shutting down.

Here are examples of other types of lists that students could develop themselves and make use of.

Line Lists: Go for a walk outdoors and have your class observe the many lines in their environment, such as the bark of a tree, spider webs, the lines on the sidewalk, the stem of a plant, the veins of a leaf, the line of buildings against the sky. Have them keep the list of lines and images as a reference for their drawings and paintings.

Interest Lists: You could have students keep lists of books read, movies seen, dates to be remembered, and famous people. They could compare their lists and find out what they have in common and where their interests differ.

4. Step In/Step Back: Looking at Pictures

A well-chosen photograph or painting can engage student interest and lead into further study. For example, when I introduced a Grade 5/6 class to *Silent to the Bone* by E.L. Konigsburg, I projected an image of "The Scream" by Edvard Munch. The impetus for choosing the painting was the first few pages of the novel, which depicts the record of a 911 emergency call. Students looked at the picture in silence. They recorded what they saw in the picture, what the picture reminded them of, and what they imagined was happening.

As a class, we talked about their individual reactions to the painting. Since the conversation seemed difficult, I asked them to return to writing and record specific detail about the painting's colors, contrast, sound, and texture. I then asked them to think of one word that could be placed in the mouth of the screamer. They were to keep it to themselves and reveal it only after we had finished reading and working with the novel.

When you want students to respond to a piece of art in a similar way, you might provide them with copies of the sheet on page 35.

Looking with a Focus: Another idea is to share pictures that have something hidden or hard to find. Students love to be challenged to find the hidden object or person. They can do this in small groups or individually. *The Mysteries of Harris Burdick* by Chris Van Allsburg is a particularly good choice for intriguing pictures.

Step In/Step Back: Looking at Pictures

I See

List the details that you see in the picture.

I Remember

Record what the painting reminds you of.

I Imagine

Imagine what is happening in the picture.

I imagine that

5. Brainstorming Ideas

Brainstorming is an opportunity for all of us to share the wealth of our knowledge and experience. It allows groups of students to generate a "pool" of ideas, examples, and questions without fear of criticism or editing. Later, groups will work with the material to explore a topic or idea in greater depth. They can expand on one another's ideas, ask questions, enter into debate about the worth of an idea and suggest alternatives; however, during the brainstorming session, students should simply generate the ideas and write them down. No criticism or editing is allowed!

I teach brainstorming by doing a Modelled Brainstorming session with the class. I underline how important it is to listen to everyone's ideas and to record them. Here is the procedure I use:

1. Appoint a recorder.
2. Appoint a timer.
3. Make sure that the recorder has a writing device and paper large enough for the group to see.
4. Make sure that everyone can see the paper or board.
5. Make sure that the timer has access to a clock or a watch.
6. Give instructions to the class.
7. Have students brainstorm for the allotted time following these rules: No editing or comments.
8. Remind students not to interrupt.
9. Have the recorder record as long as the ideas flow, but stop when the timer says to stop.
10. Provide any further instructions.

Here are two guided brainstorming sessions that work well with Junior and Intermediate students. You might try one of them as a class and then allow students to generate ideas to the problem in small groups.

Scenario for Junior students: Stephen, 11 years old, has been asked by his neighbors to take their dog out for a walk after school because they usually have to work late. The neighbors have offered to pay Stephen $8.00 per walk. He has been asked to pick the dog up from their house and return it 30 minutes later. The neighbors have asked Stephen to take the dog to the nearby park—10 minutes away—and have specifically told him *not* to let it off its leash.

Stephen has been doing the job for a week now. While he has been at the park with the dog, he has noticed that many people let their dogs off the leash so that they can play with the other dogs. The dogs seem to love the freedom. Today Stephen decides to let the dog off the leash. The dog runs to the other dogs and gets into a horrible fight. Stephen has no way of protecting the dog. The owners of the other dogs finally break the fight up and the dog is left with a bitten bleeding ear. Stephen knows that he is supposed to let the dog back into the house, but he is worried that the dog is badly hurt. He does not know what to do. Any suggestions?

Scenario for Intermediate students: Sam's parents own a variety store which is close to Sam's school. Sam works alone in the store after school. Sometimes, boys in his class come into the store and talk to him while he is working. Lately, he has noticed that little things, like candy and gum, are missing from the counter after they leave. He has never seen them take anything, but he is beginning to think that they are finding ways of distracting him and then shopliftng. His parents would be really angry about this. He thought he had a good relationship with his friends. He does not want to lose their friendship, but he wants the shoplifting to stop. What should Sam do?

6. Describing the Most Beautiful Thing You Know About

When I first began teaching pre-service teachers, I wanted to convey to them that there are a myriad of ways to open up the curriculum so that it could be mined for all sorts of possibilities. My plan was to encourage them to think of new ways to introduce subjects, themes, topics, and events to students. Before they went out on their first teaching block, I read them Richard Van Camp's book, *What's the Most Beautiful Thing You Know About Horses?* I asked them to name one of the topics that they were going to teach. Then, in a game format, I told them to approach as many students in the class as they could and ask them what the most beautiful thing about their topic was. One student asked another, "What's the most beautiful thing you know about fractions?" The student replied that the most beautiful thing that she knew about them was that they are about mystery and possibilities: that fractions are incomplete and when something is incomplete it opens us up to possibilities. Another student asked, "What's the most beautiful thing you know about ancient civilizations?" A student answered, "The most beautiful thing that I know about ancient civilizations is that when archaeologists excavate material, they consider that everything—even the most day-to-day artifacts like bowls and combs and fragments of pottery—is precious and full of memories and dreams."

Thinking in a Special Way: I once led a class where we explored a Native legend about the Star Maiden. Before I read the story to the students I asked them three questions:

What's the most **mysterious** thing you know about the sky?
What's the most **precious** thing you know about the sky?
What's the most **magnificent** thing you know about the sky?

The students wrote their responses on index cards. Here is one response:

The most mysterious thing I know about the sky is that although it can talk, it cannot tell us what to expect.

The most precious thing I know about the sky is that it gives us light and images in the day and in the night.

The most magnificent thing I know about the sky is that it is endless and full of things that we will never know about.

Here is a menu to introduce a theme or a topic to students so that they can think in new ways and ask further questions. If students are working in groups on a topic, I ask them to identify their topic at the top of the page. I hand out copies of the sheet (see pages 98–99) and ask the students to go around the room and interview as many of their peers as they can about the topic. I encourage people to "wax poetic" about the topic under consideration. I then call everyone together and ask them to share what they found out.

TOPIC: _____

- What's the most **beautiful** thing you know about _____?
- What's the most **interesting** thing you know about _____?
- What's the most **boring** thing you know about _____?
- What's the most **troubling** thing you know about _____?
- What's the most **mysterious** thing you know about _____?
- What's the most **difficult** thing you know about _____?
- What's the most **exciting** thing you know about _____?
- What's the most **dangerous** thing you know about _____?
- What's the most **tragic** thing you know about _____?
- What's the most **compelling** thing you know about _____?
- What's the most **fascinating** thing you know about _____?
- What's the most **devastating** thing you know about _____?
- What's the most **precious** thing you know about _____?
- What's the most **important** thing for us all to know about _____?

7. Who Am I? Who Are You?: Teacher in Role

I often use a strategy called "teacher in role" to intrigue students and bring them into the learning environment using their imaginations and listening skills. I tell the students that I am going to be someone else and that they are going to be people who are connected to the role that I am playing. I ask them to listen carefully for clues that will help them to understand who they are and who I am. Usually, students are intrigued by this activity and settle down to listen. Here is a good way to begin: "When I turn around, I am going to pretend to be someone other than who I am. I will carefully introduce myself and give you clues as to what my role is. I also will be letting you know in subtle ways who you are. Listen carefully for the clues that I am going to give to you. You do not have to say anything at all, but let your minds and imaginations be open to the possibilities of this dramatic encounter. When I turn back around I will be myself again, and we will talk as ourselves about who we were, where we were, what was going on in the story, and what can happen next."

I am careful to prepare for this and always keep in mind that I have to give a clear definition of *who* I am, *where* I am, and *what* is happening so that the class can begin to understand the context. I am careful to take my time and not give too much information away too early. In this way, I am introducing nuance and subtlety and helping students understand that an author spends a great deal of time leading readers into a story—leading them on so that they will want to read more.

I have used this technique hundreds of times in classrooms as I introduce themes, novels, and historical events. What appeals to students and surprises them is that the teacher is willing to shift the classroom dynamic and to give over power to them for a period of time. The role-playing unlocks new avenues of understanding and allows students to relate to the characters they are

An example of language registers:

A little boy was role-playing an ancient Greek guard. He said, "By gum, it's cold." His classmates protested, "Ancient Greeks don't talk like that." After some thought the child modified his speech to, "By ye gum, it's cold."

Dorothy Heathcote

meeting with an immediacy that is enjoyable and memorable. It also lets students practise different language registers as they speak as adults who have some authority or experience. Their roles allow them to speak in sophisticated and heightened language and to see themselves with the competencies of those roles.

On one occasion, I played the role of Ruby Bridges' mother, as presented in *Through My Eyes* by Ruby Bridges and Margo Lundell. It was the day before I sent my black six-year-old daughter to an all-white school. As the students listened to my teacher-in-role monologue, they began to understand that they were being drawn into a story of civil rights and social justice. I chose my words carefully as I spoke in role and imposed the role of Church leaders on the class.

I stopped, went out of role, and asked the students if they had any ideas about who I was and who they were. Some felt that they were "advisers" in some way. Some said they felt that they were "important," but they were not sure why. I went back into role and gave further information. The subsequent discussion about the racism that the students were facing in school and in their community was a surprise to the teacher. The role-playing had unlocked new avenues of understanding and had allowed these students to relate Mrs. Bridges' situation to their own lives and to talk about what was important to them.

Why does this strategy work? It works for many reasons. In the example above, students were placed in a position of power. I, in role as Ruby's mother, was ill at ease, worried, unsupported by my husband. I had turned to them for support and was eager to hear what they had to say. They, in role, as community leaders, were able to advise, delegate, give support, listen with empathy and concern, and have a chance to see what it feels like to be an adviser.

8. Walk Around Reading

What do I do

about the kid who's afraid to read aloud?

Howard Reynolds, an amazing teacher and consultant, taught me a wonderful strategy to get kids to read out loud. Hand out a poem that works well as a read-aloud. (Two good choices are "Say the Names" by Al Purdy and "the ghost horse of the mounties" by sean o'huigin; more titles appear in Recommended Resources at the back of the book.)

Ask the students to stand up and begin reading the text as they walk about the room. Tell them that when they get to the end of the text, they should read the poem again. Have them continue reading. Encourage them to listen to the other readers as they wander through the room. Alternatively, you might want to stagger the reading so that not everyone is reading at the same time. Start people off by touching them on the shoulder. Make sure that you do not forget anybody.

On an agreed-upon signal, have everyone stop reading and stand quietly. Ask the students to find their favorite line, phrase, or word. Tell them that when you touch them on the shoulder, you want them to say their line, phrase, or word out loud.

Create a new poetry reading by hearing these favorite lines, phrases, or words said out loud by different voices in different ways.

From Poetry to Drama: Ask the students to find partners and share their lines, phrases, or words. Have them develop a dramatic scene where only those words or lines are said out loud. The lines can be repeated, but no new lines or words can be added.

9. Playing the Applause Connection

What do I do
about the kid who derails group work and disrupts the learning in a class?

A cooperative game, such as the Applause Connection, can do more than give students practice in group work; it can build skills in cooperation and free students to become engaged in learning. As in any cooperative game, the Applause Connection provides an outlet for pent-up energy, encourages work with different people, and helps students listen to instructions. This game is particularly good for promoting improved group dynamics.

Here is how to play the game. Have students stand in a circle, and join the circle yourself. Make eye contact with the person to your left. Clap your hands. The person to your left responds to the clap by clapping back, turns to the person on her or his left, establishes eye contact, and claps once. That person claps back and then "passes the applause" to the person to her or his left. The applause is passed around the circle and comes back to you. It is really important for the students to maintain eye contact as they pass the applause. More than one clap can be sent around the circle. Encourage the exercise to go quickly and listen to suggestions from the students about how the exercise could be changed or adapted.

Once when I was working with a Grade 8 class, I could see that most of the students wanted to participate in the cooperative games I was introducing; however, a group of boys were reluctant and acted silly because the classroom bully sent them strong signals to remain uninvolved. They deferred to the bully, while the girls were sullen and discouraged, expecting the class activities to fail.

Then we played the Applause Connection, and things began to shift. Due to the kinesthetic nature of the game, the electric connection amongst the participants was visual. When all people were connecting, the game was visually appealing. The kids were amazed and said, "Wow! This is amazing!" However, when the game came to the group of boys controlled by the one kid, the connection broke down. Everyone could see the dysfunction clearly, so the pressure on those students to connect to one another and to the rest of the class was intense. Slowly, the boys began to respond to the pressure of others and began to make the game work for all.

I played that game at the beginning of each session with this class. They were amazed and then proud of how quickly they could pass the applause and became incredibly skilled at sending many different kinds of signals to one another. By the end of the fourth and final session, the electricity had crystallized in the room, and we all agreed that this form of communication had been successful. The group of boys and their leader had blended into the class and the tensions had been eliminated, at least for a while.

Of course, cooperative games are just one way in. Because bullying is essentially about power, I try to shift the power in the classroom immediately by diminishing my own power and heightening the power of the group. See "Who Am I? Who Are You?: Teacher in Role" for an example of how you might do this.

Debra Peplar, of York University, tells us that planned, consistent intervention is the best way to deal with bullying in schools. Teachers are key players and the most important thing for teachers and schools to do is to make bullying everyone's issue so that people are sensitized and willing to work to get rid of it. Many schools have anti-bullying projects and programs in place, sometimes in the form of peer mediation. Drama can help students understand the pain that accompanies bullying and cooperative games can point to the implications that bullying has for everyone.

10. Role-Playing Experts

The Experts Tell Us game provides students with authentic, although imagined contexts that demand oral language and allow for social interaction that has positive results. It is played in this way.

"Number yourselves off from 1–5. Number 1 is going to be an expert. In this case, person #1 will be an underwater diver who is an expert at finding ancient treasures. The rest of you (2, 3, 4, 5) are the owners of an international treasure hunt company. You require the expertise of an underwater diver to make a series of dangerous, but lucrative discoveries.

"I would like to speak to the experts privately. In the meantime, the members of the interviewing team should decide what qualities and expertise you would like this underwater diver to have and come up with some introductory questions. Remember to make this a formal interview and to set up the scene so that all of you will be facing the interviewee."

In a private conversation, tell the experts that they are to pretend to know as much as they can about underwater diving. Encourage them to use their imaginations and to be as serious as possible about their role. Send the experts back to their groups and then say something like "On my signal, invite the candidates to sit down and then begin the questioning."

Allow the interview to last about five minutes and then ask one interviewer per group to stand and respond to some questions, for example:

- At this point in the interview, what is your overall impression of the candidate? Are you leaning towards hiring him or her? Why or why not?
- What further questions would you like to ask before you make your decision?

Everyone in the group should have a chance to play an expert. Here are some more expert roles:

- a detective applying to an international spying agency
- an athletic coach applying to coach Olympic hopefuls
- a concert organizer applying to organize the largest concert ever
- a writer applying for the job of teen magazine editor

Generating Interest in a Novel: I have used the Experts Tell Us game to draw a Grade 8 class into the novel *Silent to the Bone*. Since the novel begins with the record of an emergency call, I invited the students to consider what qualities a

911 operator should have. Afer we developed a role on the wall (see page 50), listing words that would describe a 911 operator within a drawn figure and related roles, such as firefighter, outside of it, students formed small groups. While the "expert" 911 operators thought about their roles, group members chose roles from the list outside the figure. They also listed qualities and expertise that they thought a 911 operator should have, drafted interview questions, and set up the interview space. I provided both interviewers and candidates with assessment checklists to guide their behavior. (A sample appears as an appendix.)

Once students were about five minutes into the interviews, I interrupted to ask the interviewers some questions. The students answered my questions confidently because they felt well prepared and involved. In role, they demonstrated listening, making inferences, and synthesizing information, as well as forming and defending an opinion. For example, to answer, "Why would you be inclined to hire this candidate for the very important job of being a 911 operator?" they had to synthesize information.

Teachers know that the hard work in school—helping students to find and make meaning in texts, relationships, stories, and presentations—takes a great deal of effort on everyone's part. We know that meanings must be achieved, not found. It is important for us, as teachers, to find strategic ways to hook our students into *wanting* to know more right from the very beginning of a lesson or unit. If we do that, the momentum generated will propel all of us into further investigation and negotiation about material that matters and that students should learn about.

CHAPTER 3

Exploring the Curriculum

Education at its best is a process of teaching people to explore ideas about themselves and the world in which they live, to ask questions about the experience called living and to embrace ambiguity, to notice the unusual without fear and to look upon the ordinary with new eyes.

Maxine Greene

Opening up the curriculum for all to see...

Once you have engaged the interests and attention of your students, what kinds of activities can you do so that students remain keen to explore the material, work through the nuances, subtexts, ambiguities, and new vocabulary, think about it in new ways, and connect what they are learning to what they already know? What strategies can you continue to use to make their work provocative and interesting? You want your students to shake their fists when they read about injustice just as much as you want them to laugh when they read something funny or be able to puzzle out and analyze difficult material without giving up. You also want them to feel as if they can talk about what they are learning in a safe, supportive environment in which everyone's voice is heard.

What Helps Students Learn

Thinking: You want to encourage students to be aware that there are many different ways to look at things and to not make judgments too quickly. It helps if there is time to explore the material and to talk about it so that many different perspectives can be explored.

Talking: You want them to know that there are strategies that they can learn and practise so that they can talk about their ideas in public more easily. It helps if they have something significant to say to an audience who has a stake in their message.

Writing: You want students to know that writing is messy and challenging, and it takes time to get a finished product. It helps if they have a real reason to write and an audience who will care about what they produce.

Reading: Learning to read better is something that they can accomplish when they begin to tap into those reading strategies that are being introduced. It helps if they can experiment with different ways to read material and work with people who will support them.

Moving: We often overlook the fact that many students learn something through being physically involved. It helps if we get kids up on their feet and moving in response to a poem, a chant, something they have read, or questions that they have generated.

Working in groups: Although working in groups is often difficult, students can practise roles and responsibilities so that groups can function better. It helps if everyone understands the importance of sharing the leadership and practising group process skills.

Experimenting and risk-taking: Above all, you want your students to understand that to do something well takes time, commitment, and practice. There needs to be a willingness to explore material first. Playing with words, images, and ideas is a way to investigate what lies beneath the surface of things. Brainstorming and talking about ideas, moving to words, speaking lines in various ways and in different contexts, sketching out plans, interviewing real and imagined characters, and asking questions, such as "What if?" and "What happens when?" are some of the ways that we can explore material and thoughts to reach initial understanding.

It will take time to establish this kind of interactive work in the classroom. Time needs to be spent negotiating the rules, outlining the expectations, giving directions, explaining new vocabulary, role-modelling behavior, guiding and monitoring the practice, and helping groups work together.

The teaching strategies below provide a way to get students to experiment and take risks as they explore material that has multiple meanings and interpretations.

1. Cut to...: Creating Significant Images

Tableaux are still images, or "freeze frames," of people who freeze not only in a moment in time, but in a *problem* in time. Students can create these images with their bodies and have an opportunity to be selective as they isolate a moment of human experience that is important for them to analyze and reflect upon. This moment can come from the novel that they are reading, from a historical incident that was full of drama and suspense, from another picture that they saw in an art gallery, a book, a film, or television.

Groups of students use their bodies to create these frozen pictures that crystallize a key moment, idea, reaction, statement, or theme that the rest of the class, as the audience, can study, analyze, and discuss. This strategy requires that students work in groups to discuss, collaborate, and select the image that they want to communicate or represent. They then share this idea in complete stillness and silence.

Tableaux in Small Groups: I often teach how to make tableaux interesting to the audience before I engage in the work before us. I ask students to get into groups of three and to create tableaux such as "Baby's First Step," "An Unwanted Haircut," "Vice-Principal's Office: Late Again," "First Day in a New School," and "Freedom: The First Moment of Summer Vacation." I ask one group to volunteer as demonstrators and everyone else watches and sees how

Questions to Ask Yourself

Before the work:
- What will I have the students do?
- How will they work? (alone, in partners, in small groups, or as a whole class)
- What will I be doing as students work? (For example: observing, listening, giving further directions, teaching new skills, monitoring progress, side-coaching, demonstrating, facilitating, challenging assumptions)
- How am I going to ensure that the groups function effectively?
- What rules and expectations should I remind them of?

After the work:
- Did I use the right teaching strategy?
- What other strategies might have worked better?
- Did the students have enough knowledge and experience to do the work?

effective the strategy can be. Then the whole class works in their groups of three.

I ask students to think about and experiment with

- different levels—high, medium, low—so that the image is varied in form
- various body shapes—open, closed
- the relationship in terms of physical distance between and amongst the characters in the tableau
- what the audience will focus on when the tableau is presented and
- different kinds of emotions, body language, and facial expression

They need to make sure that the important elements in the tableau can be seen by the rest of the class when the image is shared.

Whole-class "Crowd Scenes": Sometimes, students are willing to participate in tableaux, but are uncomfortable about being "exposed" in a small group. In this exercise, the students work as a whole class. Everyone must participate and cooperate with one another.

Have the students stand as a class facing you. Tell them that they are going to create three tableaux representing a series of events that tell a story with a distinct beginning, middle, and end. They are to think of these images as something that they might see on the 6 p.m. evening news. They should work together in silence, be aware of what is happening, and adjust to what others are doing.

You might say something like this: "I'm going to ask you to work together to create a tableau of an accident at the corner of a busy intersection in a town or city. Remember that all of you must be involved in creating the picture. There needs to be a focus to the picture, use of three different levels, and roles for everyone. Some of you could be bystanders, reporters, police or ambulance workers. Of course there needs to be a victim or victims, but let that happen spontaneously as you work in silence. When I say, 'cut to...' I am going to ask you to create another scene that will happen later. Let's try to create the first tableau."

"Accident"
        cut to
                "Hospital Operating Room"
                        cut to
                                "Joyous Recovery"

Work with the students, having them practise moving effortlessly between scenes so that the story can be told smoothly and efficiently. Once they have mastered the "cut to..." strategy as a whole class, they can try it in small groups.

Transforming Images: The thought-provoking poem "Southern Mansion," by the black writer and academic Arna Bontemps, lends itself to the fluid creation of tableaux. (See page 46.) Your class might imagine that a film director is going to begin a film using the text of this poem as the opening sequence. What sounds and images would the director likely bring to life?

To explore this question with the class, read the poem aloud and then read it again, this time with students keeping their eyes shut. Encourage them to imagine the setting and the sounds that are part of the poem. After the reading, have a discussion about what students saw and heard. What images did they find most powerful?

Divide the class into two equal groups and have each group work on opposite sides of the classroom. Ask one group to create the images of the southern mansion and the other to create an image of what would be happening "in the field."

Next, have each group decide how the past has changed into the present. Tell them to transform their tableau from the past into one set in the present using the "cut to..." strategy. Invite them to share their transformations with one another and talk about what was represented.

Southern Mansion

Poplars are standing there still as death
And ghosts of dead men
Meet their ladies walking
Two by two beneath the shade
And standing on the marble steps.

There is a sound of music echoing
Through the open door
And in the field there is
Another sound tinkling in the cotton:
Chains of bondmen dragging on the ground.

The years go back with an iron clank,
A hand is on the gate,
A dry leaf trembles on the wall.
Ghosts are walking.
They have broken roses down
And poplars stand there still as death.

Have them explore images in different ways. They can capture the image that the public sees and then capture the image that is the truth.

Here are two ways of applying the "cut to..." strategy.

Picture Book	Novel
Example: *The Invisible Princess*, by Faith Ringold	Example: *The Giver*, by Lois Lowry (Jonas becomes aware of a different reality as he spends time with the "Receiver of Memories," or the Giver.)
Favorite scene #1 *cut to* (a narrator uses transitional words, such as *but* and *however*.)	
	Memory #1 *cut to*
Favorite scene #2 *cut to*	Memory #2 *cut to*
Favorite scene #3	Memory #3

2. Step Out and Say Something

Tableaux can provide the base from which students interpret events or text, write, and speak.

Improvising What to Say: This approach works particularly well with historical themes. For example, if students were exploring the sixteenth-century immigration of young brides-to-be to the New World—*les filles du roi*—they could first create a tableau about their departure from France; they could then step out of the tableau to speak as the historical characters they represent. Within an integrated lesson, they might convey the journey on board ship across the Atlantic Ocean as a soundscape. An effective way to show their arrival in New France (Quebec) would be, first, to have students create a tableau showing the women and male settlers facing one another for the first time and then, to touch students on the shoulder to speak in role. Improvising, they should explain who they are and what they are thinking and feeling.

Later, students could write down what they said, enhance it, and then re-create the sequence, which will be much richer.

Sharing Images and Lines: Alternatively, students could create a tableau based on an excerpt of text and interpret the text. Divide up the lines of text so that everyone in the tableau has something to say. Rehearse the piece so that everyone knows his or her cues. Form the tableau, and when it's their turn, students break out of the formation, say their lines, and then go back into the tableau.

3. Put Yourself on the Line

Conflict, confusion, and crisis are all part of the human condition. Critical moments in literature, history, science, sports, and the arts can be brought into the classroom in a way that makes learning exciting.

Making a choice or acting without thinking always has consequences. Great leaders, athletes, and movie stars have all made errors of judgment. Students find these moments fascinating if they become involved in the narrative in a way that makes them realize the importance of these moments, which may be full of suspense, disappointment, hilarity, sadness, mystery, and unanswered questions. They begin to wonder what propelled people into doing what they did. Moments of indecision, ambivalence, and vacillation are the stuff that makes life troubling, but interesting to students.

Take an issue and invite students to respond in one of these three ways:

- Stand on this side of the line if you believe that...
- Stand on the other side of the line if you believe that...
- Stand in the middle if you do not want to make a decision at this time or if you feel that you need more information.

Often, students are able to explain, argue, and defend their opinions if they see that they have indeed taken a stand. If they are standing among people who hold the same opinions that they do, they can confer with them, talk about the issue, and prepare to defend their opinions before they are asked to do so to the whole class.

Reacting in Role: As mentioned earlier, I have worked with the poem "South-ern Mansion" (see page 46), asking students to create tableaux about what the mansion looked like in the past and in the present. I followed up by asking students to imagine that they were ghosts of people who had once worked at the mansion. They were invited to stand close to the building if they felt that they would want to return or further away from it if their memories made them not want to return. I prompted them to think about what they would probably see, feel, remember, and hear. They froze into positions related to their charac-ters, prepared to speak in role when tapped on the shoulder.

In another instance, when I explored the topic of immigration, I asked students to decide how keen they were to come to Canada. They were to stand close to the line if they wanted to immigrate and far from it if they were reluc-tant to. They were required to give reasons for where they were standing.

4. Experimenting with Choral Speaking

Choral speaking and chanting involve experimentation, interpretation, and rehearsal of a piece of text, for example, a poem or riddle. The students can discuss the meaning of the text and consider who might be speaking and to whom. They can experiment with the language, exploring rhythm, cadence, volume, and pace. Some parts of the text may be read solo and some in unison with either the whole group or a part of the group. Chanting a short rhyme is a good way to begin.

What do I do about the kid who is reluctant to read out loud?

Reading Out Loud as a Whole Class: Have the class stand in a circle and hand out copies of the text chosen. Have students read the text silently to themselves. On a signal, begin reading the text in unison. Tell the students that they are going to read the poem again, but this time each person will say one line. One person in the circle will read the first line and the person next to him or her will read the next line. The reading will go around the circle until everyone has had a turn reading or the poem is finished (whichever comes first.) Encourage students to pay attention to how the poem sounds—how different kinds of voices saying the lines in different ways changes the impact of the poem.

All Together Now: Prepare for a choral reading by first having students read the text aloud to themselves as they wander around the room. This Walk Around Reading strategy is outlined in Chapter 2. Invite the students to choose their favorite lines, phrases, or words and then find peers who made the same choices. In groups, have students discuss why they made the choices they did. Have them practise reading their lines, phrases, or words in unison. Orchestrate a reading of the text. Ask for volunteers to read the lines that were not chosen. Read the text again, asking for suggestions about how to combine the voices so that the effect gets better and better. The goal is for the text to be read by the whole class without hesitation and with great impact.

Combining Choral Speaking with Image Making: Reread the text or poem again, this time inviting the students to say their lines and then move into frozen images that encapsulate those lines. The text can be read in a circle and become a choral reading with movement.

I once worked with a Grade 4/5 class to present "Remember the Bridge" by Carole Boston Weatherford. The poem has eight stanzas and each group was responsible for finding a way to read their part of the poem. The class worked on the lines and then found a way to walk into tableaux that represented the text. Once they were in a tableau, students read their parts chorally, then the image cut to that of the next group. The whole class came together to read and represent the final stanza:

THE JOURNEY CONTINUES (walk out of original tableaux groups and come to the front)
THE BRIDGE STILL HOLDS STRONG (everyone holds right hand up in a fist)
HANDS REACH ACROSS WATER (everyone brings right hand down, palms up, and reaches out to the audience)
HEARTS SING A NEW SONG (everyone puts hands on their hearts and looks up and out)

The following poem, "Night in Al-Hamra" was written by Saadi Youssef and translated from the Arabic by Khaled Mattawa. It is good source material for choral speaking combined with image making.

Night in Al-Hamra

A candle on the long road
A candle in the slumbering houses
A candle for the terrified stores
A candle for the bakeries
A candle for the journalist shuddering in an empty office
A candle for the fighter
A candle for the doctor at the sick bed
A candle for the wounded
A candle for honest talk
A candle for the staircases
A candle for the hotel crowded with refugees
A candle for the singer
A candle for the broadcasters in a shelter
A candle for a bottle of water
A candle for the air
A candle for two lovers in a stripped apartment
A candle for the sky that has folded
A candle for the beginning
A candle for the end
A candle for the final decision
A candle for my conscience
A candle in my hand

What do I do
about the kid who finds it hard to make meaning from text?

5. Working with Material Visually

Graphic organizers, including the familiar Venn diagram and maps, are useful in helping some students wrestle with the meaning of texts; the motivations of characters; timelines; the settings and contexts of novels, stories, and plays; and other kinds of material. These students benefit from working with material in a visual way. Below are a few specific ways of exploring a topic visually.

Thumbnail Sketches: Students may do a thumbnail sketch of what they imagine a place to look like. I once asked Grade 6 students who had been reading the novel *Wringer* to make a sketch of Palmer's bedroom. Where was the window where the pigeon came to call? Where was the closet where Palmer hid the pigeon? Where were the bed, the lamp, the dresser, and the desk? Where was the door? The students shared their sketches with one another and compared how their imaginations had taken them into the story and into the room. Sometimes, it is a good idea to have the class make a collective drawing on mural paper.

Role on the Wall: I first encountered role on the wall in a workshop conducted by Jonothan Neelands and have used this strategy hundreds of times in different ways. First, have a volunteer draw a large abstract diagram representing a character on the chalkboard. Ask students to record words that describe the character on the inside of the figure. For example, if they were reading the picture book *The Woman Who Outshone the Sun*, they could record words that describe the woman's characteristics in her long, flowing magical hair. You could also ask students, on the outside of the figure, to identify the pressures that the character is facing. People who are supportive of the character could be listed around the figure.

You can use roles on the wall for comparing and contrasting characters. For example, when I worked with a Grade 4 class on *When Jessie Came Across the Sea*, the students created two roles on the wall: one for Jessie and another for her grandmother. We used them to explore the similarities of their feelings about being separated and the differences between their experiences.

One Grade 7 class went further. Students compared the characteristics of the bullies with those of the victims in *Wringer* through the strategy. As they continued to listen to the book being read to them by their teacher, they added words and ideas within the figures. They could see what the bullies and victims had in common. When it came time to do their retell, relate, and reflect work as part of the reading lesson, they were able to refer to the graphic images easily.

Responses Within Shapes: Students could respond to poetry within an image of their own choosing. For example, they could write poetry on war in a bomb shape, poetry on nature in a tree shape, and poetry on the future in a star shape.

6. Working with Scripts

Starting lines, minimal scripts, and monologues all offer ways of exploring scripts.

Starting Lines: Students can use a starting line and quickly get a response from their partners. You might want to do a demonstration in front of the class so that the students understand that a line alone can propel people into a relationship that is interesting to watch. Ask for someone to be a volunteer. Have that person respond with one line only. For instance, if you say, "Don't ever say that to me again!" the respondent could simply say, "What?" You then have a minimal script that can have all sorts of meanings and subtexts. Here are some other starting lines:

- Why do you continue to do this to me and my family?
- May I borrow that for a few days?
- Please give me another chance. Please.
- I have told you I don't have time to see you now.
- Promise me that you will never tell.

Minimal Scripts: Have students work in pairs and explore the following minimal scripts.

Do you have to go there again?
Yes.
Well, fine, then.

Why did you have to say that?
What?
It's always this way.

I swear that I didn't mean to do it.
Yeah?
I swear.

I have been meaning to ask you something.
What?
Oh, never mind.

Are you going to tell her?
I don't know. Do you think I should?
It's not for me to say.

I don't know why it always has to end up this way.
What does?
This.

Tell me everything is going to be all right.
I can't do that.
Why not?

Ask students to read each script silently and then to decide who is going to read which lines. Have them read the script aloud. Prompt them to discuss *who* could be saying the lines, *where* the characters could be, and *what* is really happening in the scene. Next, with these understandings in place, have them read the scene again. Ask them to switch roles. Do they think that doing this changes the meaning in any way?

Monologue: As a longer speech, or soliloquy, a monologue offers opportunities for students to explore a character's thoughts and feelings in greater detail. The sample monologue provided below appears in Michael Miller's play *In the Freedom of Dreams*. It expresses the concerns of one woman.

Everyday I get up at four o'clock in the morning. I comb my daughter's hair while she is still asleep so that it will look nice for school the next day. I make breakfast for the children and by quarter to five I am waiting at the bus stop to go to work. By the time the bus arrives at my stop it is already full. I stand in the aisle for an hour and a half. That is how long it takes me to get to the back door of my madam's house. I get her children out of bed. I make them breakfast. I clean the house. I make the madam breakfast. I do the laundry. I clean some more. I iron the clothes. I make lunches. I cook dinner. If I am lucky I can get home in time to see my children off to bed. Most nights I am not that lucky. I spend one full day with my children each week. Only Sunday.

The fares for the buses are high. If these fares rise then I will not be able to take the bus to work. I will have to live in the madam's house or be fired. Jobs are hard to find. If I have to live in who will look after my children for me? Who is going to comb my little girl's hair for school?

Have the students read the monologue silently, and then invite them to work with a partner. One person reads the first line; the partner reads the second line. They continue in this fashion until they finish the piece. Prompt the students to find the most poignant line in the monologue. Ask them to find a way to represent that line in a still image or tableau. They can bring the image to life for a second as they say the line. The students could take the monologue further by generating a list of questions that they would like to ask the woman and using the questions to begin research on Nelson Mandela and apartheid in South Africa.

7. Speaking in Role

Speaking in role requires participants in drama to

- be aware of their environment and their relationship with others
- change language registers to meet the demands of the role
- "live through" the situation, that is, speak words that are relevant to the situation and period in time and show no advance knowledge of what will occur as a result of their actions

Because drama is concerned with the crises, or turning points, of life, large and small, which cause people to reflect and take note, speaking in role requires students to modify and give form to their ideas, expressions, and sentiments in "heated," not cold circumstances. It allows students to find oral language easily.

Speaking in role can happen in many ways in the classroom:

- through games, such as Experts Tell Us (see pages 41–42)
- in paired, small-group, and large-group improvisations where the teacher presents dramatic situations and the students take on roles
- when the teacher in role imposes roles on the students and guides, monitors, and deepens the students' response from within the drama (see pages 38–39)
- when students read a text and then re-enact the situation(s) in and beyond the text through role-playing
- when students take on roles in choral reading and Readers Theatre (see pages 48–49 and 61–63)
- when students read the roles of characters in a dramatic script

The techniques of drama centre on transformation: how people can turn into other people or other beings in order to create a there and then story in a here and now place.

Richard Schecter

8. A Bird's Eye View: I See, I Wonder, I Hope

This writing strategy allows students to break down their feelings and thoughts into three sections. It offers them a way to be objective, then imaginative, and finally reflective about what they are learning. The structure makes the writing task more manageable and helps those students who have difficulty organizing their thoughts to tackle the job more confidently. I use this strategy in various contexts to help students organize their feelings and thoughts so that effective discussion can happen as a whole class, in groups, or in partners. The strategy also allows students to gain some distance from the material that they are considering. It affords them an opportunity to experience what it is like to be a "fly on the wall" or to have a "bird's eye view."

If students are looking at historical incidents or characters in novels, they can situate themselves as observers. The strategy allows them to record what they know, to ask questions about what they want to know, and to go into the realm of feeling response.

When I was reading *Wringer* to a group of Grade 5 students, I asked them to imagine what the day of the pigeon shoot looked and felt like from a distance. I asked them to record their own feelings about the event in the final paragraph. Here is one student's response.

> I see a day that is hot and filled with thousands of people who do not know what they are doing. They have no feelings for the pigeons and they are being destructive to the world in ways that are beyond imagining. I see the pigeons being let out of their cages and I have to look away.

> I wonder whether any of the pigeons ever get a feeling the day before this happens that something is going to go horribly wrong. I wonder if they try to escape. I wonder what the pigeons are fed the night before the shoot and if some of them don't eat because they know that things are not right. If I lived in this town I would sneak out at night and open all the cages and let the pigeons fly free!

> I hope that this kind of thing does not really happen in real life. It is very difficult to believe that a whole town of people would be so violent and uncaring. I hope that Palmer finds a way of protecting Nipper from the bullies that are his so-called friends and the adult bullies who organize the pigeon shoot. They are just wrong, wrong, wrong!!!!!

9. Getting Past the Words

Exploring voice, movement, and sound can help students feel more comfortable in dealing with and understanding texts with challenging language.

Word Discoveries: One strategy that works with students is to have them play with the language in difficult texts so that they gain confidence and can then persevere when they encounter difficulties while reading independently. Have them work with famous quotations or with excerpts from the text that they are reading. Ask them to

- read the quotations silently to themselves
- circle all the words that they do not know

What do I do about the kid who has trouble connecting with text because the language seems intimidating?

- underline the words that they think are old fashioned and not used much anymore
- guess what some of the words mean
- compare their assumptions with those of other people in their groups
- take turns looking up the words in a dictionary and sharing the meanings with group members and
- record all of the words for which there were no definitions

In one instance, I helped students make word discoveries while working with a Grade 5 teacher to team-teach *The Midwife's Apprentice* by Karen Cushman. While showing the class the front cover of the novel, I asked them what the artist had done to help them see that the story would be set in the past. The students talked about the strange hat that the person on the cover was wearing. I told them it was called a "wimple," which they thought was a very funny word! I said we would be discovering other words in the novel that were "old" and asked them to be ready to hear or read those words and to remain curious about them. Some of the words might not even be in the dictionary so we would have to find other ways of learning what the words meant.

I wanted to give students an idea that learning unfamiliar words might be worth the trouble. I gave each group of three a brief quote by William Shakespeare. I told the students that all these lines were written in plays and sonnets by the famous sixteenth-century playwright. The lines are kept alive by actors who perform in plays that are seen and heard by audiences all over the world. They have been translated into many different languages, including German, Japanese, and Swedish.

After students went through the process of exploring words outlined above, we talked about our "word discoveries" and shared our new knowledge. Groups of three then stood in straight lines and read the quotes out loud in unison. They said them in various ways: loudly, in whispers, with great melodrama, stiffly, like robots. Next, I invited students to think of who said the line, where they could be, and what was really happening. The students said their quotes and then froze in tableaux. We discussed how all the scenes portrayed something sad and students were encouraged to remember these images as the teacher began reading the novel. They were asked to listen for various kinds of words, such as those recorded in the chart below.

She looks on tempests and is never shaken.

Shakespearean sonnet

Grief fills the room of my absent child.

King John, Act 3, Scene 3

Such perilous stuff weighs upon my heart.

Macbeth, Act 5, Scene 3

Desolate, desolate.
Will I hence and die?

King Richard II, Act 1, Scene 2

Tears do not stop the floodgates of her eyes.

Henry IV, Part 1, Act 2, Scene 4

Hast thou not dropped from heaven?

The Tempest, Act 2, Scene 2

I shall miss thee, but yet thou shalt have freedom.

The Tempest, Act 5, Scene 1

But woe is me, you are so sick of late,
so far from cheer and from your former state,
that I distrust you.

Hamlet, Act 3, Scene 2

Unfamiliar words	Alliterative words	Old words	Repetition
moiling	taunted and tormented	morrow	unwashed, unnourished, unloved, unlovely
stench	and kept her waking and walking and working	wimple	she dreamed of nothing, hoped for nothing, expected nothing
heedless		mistress	
scavenged			

Soundscape: Alternatively, you can use a strategy that allows students to experiment with different ways to create the sounds of a scene. They can use voice, body percussion, found objects, and simple instruments. Have the students work in groups. Let students experiment with volume, pace, tone, and timing to find the most effective combination of sounds that will represent what they are trying to say.

I have used this strategy many times as we investigate and interpret poems and other texts that have sound and image in them. It also works well as a way to get into historical incidents that evoke sound and image. What might your students do with something like this?

"Hundreds of people, men, women and children...huddled together without light, without air, wallowing in filth...sick in body, dispirited in heart...washing was impossible...the voyage took three months."

10. Saying It Through Movement

What do I do

about the kid who has trouble expressing ideas in words or on paper?

Some students find it easier to tell what they understand through their bodies. Through movement, they can effectively share, represent, and communicate their ideas. In the exercise outlined below, students engage in movement in groups of four. A large, open space is required so that they can experiment with their ideas.

Ask each group to decide on four words or ideas related to the text that they are reading. Tell them that they are going to represent what they would like to say through movement. They could take four words from a role on the wall (see page 50) or pull images from the piece of text. They might choose words that relate to one another or ones that can be juxtaposed to cause a certain effective jaggedness to their work.

Once group members have decided on the words or ideas, have them "body storm" various ways to interpret them through movement. Coach them as they work: tell them to change levels, move at different speeds and in different ways, alter relationships, and "travel the movement." Let the groups explore the various words until they have set the movements and the sequence that they would like to share.

Next, students prepare to move to music. They number themselves off in their small groups and organize themselves in a diamond formation. Person #1, the first leader, faces a wall or window and the other students face the same way. The students will likely find that slow music is best because the movements can be sustained and the group members can follow one another and make transitions more easily.

As person #1 begins to move, the other students shadow, or mirror, the movement. After a time, the leader rotates to the right and the other group members follow the rotation. Now they mirror the movements initiated by person #2, then person #3 and then person #4 until their interpretation of the theme, image, character, or concept is finished.

Choreography Based on Role on the Wall: At a dramatic arts conference with 120 students, we explored the story of Lucia Zenteno as told in the picture book *The Woman Who Outshone the Sun*. The students generated words to describe the character and her predicament. In the centre of an outline of the figure, they described Lucia's character: strong, caring, empathetic, proud, silent, magical. On the outside of the figure, they wrote words to describe the problems that she faced before the villagers drove her away: discrimination, racism, bullying, fear, hatred, misunderstanding, division, and more. Each group of students chose four words from those that the whole group had generated and created breathtaking choreography to music.

Since the pressures on teachers to "cover the curriculum" are enormous, it is often tempting to revert to more traditional ways of teaching to convey information. It is important that teachers hang on to the understanding that students construct their own knowledge and learn about things as they work with the information and do something with it. Students, therefore, need to be given time to make personal connections with the material by becoming actively involved with it. Everyone brings different perspectives, so lots of time needs to be spent working with personal reactions to and interpretations of the material presented.

...to teach is not to transfer knowledge but to create the possibilities for the production or construction of knowledge.

Paulo Freire

CHAPTER 4

Extending the Learning

Teaching is a matter of awakening and empowering today's young people to name, to reflect, to imagine, and to act with more and more concrete responsibility in an increasingly multifarious world. At once, it is a matter of enabling them to remain in touch with dread and desire, with the smell of lilacs and the taste of a peach. The light may be uncertain and flickering; but teachers in their lives and works have the remarkable capacity to make it shine in all sorts of corners and, perhaps, to move newcomers to join with others and transform.

Maxine Greene

As teachers it is our responsibility to help students to watch more carefully, see more fully and think more deeply. This means that they have to be responsive to nuance, subtlety, and subtext. We want students to be open to the unexplored possibilities in texts, in classroom relationships, in experiences, and in problems to be solved and thought about. We can get them to notice things and be open to new thoughts and perspectives only if we model this kind of behavior in the classroom and remain determined to make learning not just a series of exercises to be completed, but a series of profound and authentic experiences to be analyzed and reflected on in exciting and stimulating ways. As teachers, we need to model thoughtfulness and push ourselves to look beyond the surface of things, of people both in the present and in the past, of their complex relationships with others and with property and power. We need to be careful about making quick judgments about people and events and demonstrate thoughtful analysis and risk-taking as ways of finding out about the world. I always value *not* knowing as a perfect place to begin.

The Teacher's Role in Furthering Understandings

Unfortunately, some students have been conditioned to think that there are right and wrong answers to what they are learning. Fearful that they do not know the right answer, they do not take part fully in class discussions and projects. They do not want to appear to be wrong. As they get older, the thought of being embarrassed becomes even more of a worry and the pressure from their peers for them to speak and behave in ways acceptable to them is intense. These students lack confidence and begin to second-guess what they are going to do and say.

How do you begin to deepen the learning experience for students? I like to think of this part of work in classrooms as "putting our knowledge to work." We want to get kids to make the learning their own, have the confidence to ask questions, and find connections to their lives and to the other things that they are learning. It is time for them to learn how to present their understandings in new and exciting ways, and as they do so, they begin to gain self-confidence, group process skills, thoughtfulness, and a desire to learn more.

Teachers need to play many different roles at this stage of the learning process—guide, facilitator, connector of ideas, research assistant, and more—so that students are stimulated to think, to find out more, and to tell us what they are learning and thinking about. I always frame my teaching around these questions: "What do I want them to see? to experience? to know? to feel? to think about? to imagine? to remember?"

Ten activities or strategies that encourage students to deepen their understanding are outlined in the balance of the chapter.

1. Creating Questions to Deepen Understanding

"The brother died and then the sister died" tells a story that makes us curious. "First, the brother and then the sister died of grief" is a story that forces us to immediately ask questions. What happened that made these two people so sad that they both died? Could they have died of broken hearts? Is it possible for that to happen? What does this story reminds us of? How can we find out more?

In my teaching, I often set up situations in which students have an opportunity to ask questions that will deepen their understanding of texts, behaviors, and relationships. In this work, I have been influenced by Juliana Saxton and Norah Morgan, as well as Kathleen Gallagher. In order for students to become critical thinkers and independent learners, they need to know how to ask questions that will further their understanding. We need to give students opportunities to practise asking open-ended questions that are the outcome of knowledge and thought. We can ask "what happens if" and get one kind of answer, and then we can ask, "What happens when" and get another kind of answer.

In their book, *Asking Better Questions*, Norah Morgan and Juliana Saxton present three categories of questions:

- Questions that elicit information
  For example: What was the name of the town in which Winnie Foster lived?
- Questions that shape understanding
  For example: Was it just coincidence that...?
- Questions that press for reflection
  For example: What kind of preparation does a person have to have in order to stand up to injustice and risk physical or emotional hurt?

After students have begun working on a project, unit, novel, or any other kind of endeavor I often stop the work and ask these questions:

- What do we know?
- What do we want to know?
- Where can we go to find out?
- How does that relate to...?
- What further questions can we ask to open up the topic in a new way?

2. May There Be...

A familiar maxim is that we should write about what we know. As poet Michael Rosen observes, for some children that means not being powerful. I have students write about what is going on in their lives: moving from one house to another, getting in trouble, having a curfew, not being allowed to do things, being treated unfairly, being jealous. They can also write about their fears and worries. Doing this allows them to achieve what Rosen sees as the three purposes of writing:

- to preserve things
- to reflect on experiences and ideas that you are reading or talking about
- to open up a conversation about what is important

There are several ways to get students to read their writing. Some students derive deep pleasure from hearing their peers' writing read aloud. Some are terrified at the prospect of reading it. I find that it helps if you have students read their writing to a partner first. The partner can comment and give some feedback. You can encourage the students to say positive things and then make one suggestion for possible improvement. If the partners combine their writing into a short reading, they have a reason to work together to critique each other's work. They can find a way of combining some parts of their writing so that there is a mingling of words, phrases, and ideas read by two voices.

Here is one good way to help students turn their writing into reading. Hand out index cards and have the class listen to the song "Oh, what a wonderful world." Ask them to record the words, images, flavors, ideas, thoughts, and connections that they are making as they listen to the lyrics on one side of the cards. After the music has finished, ask them to turn their cards over. At the top of the other side of the cards, they write:

MAY THERE BE...

On the bottom of the cards, they write:

MAY THERE NOT BE...

The students then find a way to write the endings of the two sentence fragments from the words, images, flavors, ideas, thoughts, and connections recorded on the other side of their cards.

One Grade 5 student wrote this poem:

MAY THERE BE...
flowers in every spring
MAY THERE BE...
rainbows that go on forever
MAY THERE BE...
people who care

MAY THERE NOT BE...
bombs that explode
MAY THERE NOT BE...
fractured promises
MAY THERE NOT BE...
bullies who get away with it

What do I do
about the kid who is
worried about sharing
writing aloud?

The students then find ways of combining their writing so that it becomes a script of sorts. They practise reading their writing aloud and adjust their artistic decisions so that the reading works in a dramatic way. They can explore a menu of different ways to combine their writing and the reading of their writing. I generally present this menu: repeating words and phrases; sharing voices; echoing; standing back to back, face to face, or side to side; using high and low levels; and adding movement and gesture.

The students decide where they want to present their readings within the classroom. When I do this exercise with students, I have them stand in their pairs. I simply walk past a pair and nod, and they begin their reading. We very quickly put together an ensemble piece.

You might end this session with a reading of John Marsden's *Prayer for the 21st Century* so that the students can see and hear their poetry juxtaposed with the beautiful poetry in the picture book. If you have time, you could work with the class to see how you could interweave their writing with the text of the book or use the text as a model for their writing.

A Grade 8 class that was preparing a presentation for their graduation ceremony used *Prayer for the 21st Century* as a model for their writing. Here is an excerpt from their final script:

> May there be good times to remember
> And memories that last day to day
> May we all be models for others
> And practice what to do and to say
> May those who came from a distance
> Remember those who remain
> May peace run throughout our existence
> And friendship course through our veins

3. Inner/Outer Circle

Inner/outer circle works because it is theatrical and allows the teacher to orchestrate the reading of students' writing and create the effect that everyone's voice is heard. The group of students in the inner circle sits and the group of students in the outer circle stands. If, for instance, you have had the students write in role, they can read their writing from two different perspectives.

I have used this strategy with *Silent to the Bone*. I had half the students write in role as Bramwell, and they wrote a *diary account* of their first impressions of the detention centre. I had the other half of the class write in role as the case worker, and they wrote *a report* about their first impressions of Bramwell when he entered the detention centre. As I touched the students on the shoulder to signal that they should read their writing, we heard different voices and different genres interplay with one another. The effect was astounding. Because I could stop the reading at any point and return to the different readers, I could manipulate the effect. Weaker and stronger writers had opportunities to play off one another. Here is what the reading sounded like.

Bramwell 1: Dear Diary: I can't believe that this has happened to me. Everything in my world has changed completely since the 911 call...

Case worker 1: September 12, 2003; Gender: Male; Height: 5 foot 2; Weight: Approximately 105 lb. Entry time: 12:01. Brought in by police. Looks terrified. Parents arrive later.

Bramwell 2: This is the worst day of my life. I am in a cell with one other person. I am cold and tired and frightened. I was brought here by my "case worker," who seems nice, but the way I am feeling I don't trust anyone anymore.

Case worker 2: The boy did not speak to me or to anyone else even though I asked him a number of questions in order to write this report. I think that he needs time. He seems to have been through a lot in the past few hours.

Bramwell 1: Dear Diary: I can't believe that this has happened to me. Everything in my world has changed completely since the 911 call...

Case worker 4: I don't know what to do to comfort him.

Bramwell 3: One thing that I have decided is that I will not speak until I can be sure that I will be heard and that my story will be believed.

Case worker 3: Report submitted at the end of my shift. Bramwell is sleeping now. He has not eaten, but did drink water at 10:00 p.m. He still has not spoken.

Bramwell 4: Dear Diary: I have been allowed to write in a diary so they have given me sheets of paper to write on. I...

Bramwell 1: Dear Diary: I can't believe that this has happened to me. Everything in my world has changed completely since the 911 call...

Case worker 4: I don't know what to do to comfort him.

4. A Corridor of Voices

What makes this reading-your-writing strategy work well is the physical placement of the students in a gauntlet and the suspense of wondering what decision a character will make. Students read opinions that they have expressed in writing as a volunteer in character moves down a corridor of facing lines of students. Perhaps representing the conscience of the character, they express a range of thoughts, feelings, perspectives, and options that need to be considered. In *Tuck Everlasting*, for example, Winnie Foster has to decide whether or not to drink the water from the spring that would give her everlasting life. On her seventeenth birthday, she goes to the spring. What decisions should she make after listening to what a corridor of voices has to say? This activity might help a student who is unclear about what to write and needs ideas to begin.

5. Interpreting Text in Readers Theatre

*What do I do
about the kid who is
reluctant to read out loud?*

Readers Theatre is an excellent way to draw students into reading. Reluctant readers often find that they are needed to speak in unison with others, make sound effects with their voices, repeat words or phrases, or read the part of a solo character. Readers Theatre provides students with an authentic reason to engage in repeated reading of texts. It helps students attend to the meaning of the material they are reading and involves them in a positive, social reading activity in which risk-taking, experimentation, modelling, instruction, and feedback are natural components of rehearsals.

Students work in groups made up of readers of different abilities. They may work with various kinds of texts, such as stories, jokes, poems, or excerpts from novels or famous speeches. A favorite source of mine is *The Iron Man* by Ted Hughes. As students prepare to perform, they read the text many times in different ways, experimenting with different roles and combinations of voices. They gain confidence as they do this.

Students do not have to memorize their parts; indeed, they should be seen to be reading. However, all readers are expected to follow the text, know their cues and parts, and rehearse the piece many times with the group so that their performance is fluid. Readers Theatre does not usually involve costumes, set, or movement. The readers generally stand while reading, using their voices to bring the action of the scene to life in the imaginations of their audience.

In a November 2002 article in *The Reading Teacher*, Jo Worthy and Kathryn Prater recorded this instance of the value of Readers Theatre:

> One boy's story is typical of what happens when resistant readers participate in Readers Theatre. That fourth grader, reading more than two years below grade level, put reading at the top of his not-to-do list. According to his teacher, he never chose to read on his own: during free reading time his attention wandered. Despite the teacher's sincere and skillful attempts, the boy remained apathetic about reading. During the spring, the teacher started a unit on Readers Theatre. She predicted that he would not be enthusiastic, not only because of his dislike of reading, but because he was introverted and reserved. Fortunately she was wrong. The first set of scripts that she used were based on Marc Brown's Arthur series (e.g. *Arthur's Birthday*, 1991). The teacher allowed the students to choose the script they wanted to perform and the students negotiated how to choose the parts in their groups. Not surprisingly, the boy chose the part with the fewest lines (two), and the group began preparing for the performance. At the end of the day, he asked if he could take home one of the scripts to read with his cousin. Trying to hide her shock, the teacher handed him several copies to take with him. The next day the boy came to school reading his part perfectly and even with a hint of expression. As the unit progressed he began to request "the biggest part" and to become his character in the performances. Readers Theatre made an amazing difference in that student's motivation to read on his own, in his comfort level in the classroom, and ultimately in his reading proficiency. The teacher's only regret was that she had not begun using Readers Theatre sooner.

Presenting Favorite Stories: I recommend older students performing for younger grades, working and experimenting with ways to read picture books. When I was a teacher in a secondary school my Grade 12 students would write and perform Readers Theatre for younger audiences as their Children's Theatre unit. Usually, they performed for Grade 7 or 8 audiences; occasionally, for primary students.

First, we would visit the feeder schools and find out what the students' favorite books were. Then, we would go to the library, research the material, and put together a number of Readers Theatre performances that we would present to the classes. We did not worry about props and costumes. We just worked the material so that the students could "see" all of these details in their imaginations. We were always fascinated by the letters and drawings that we received from these students when they wrote us thank-you letters. They had "seen" so much and yet all my students had done was to read the words in such a way that the texts came alive.

Interpreting Historical Documents: Perhaps the most profound experience I had using Readers Theatre was when I was asked by the senior administration of the Toronto Board of Education to present something of a dramatic nature for the board's final meeting. (The board was one of seven boards of education that were being amalgamated.) I worked with a Grade 8 class. The kids and I visited the archives at the Toronto Board of Education. We were allowed to look at the original minutes of the first board meeting 150 years earlier. I watched the students look in awe at how the minutes had been written out by quill pen. What was just as fascinating was the content of the minutes. We took turns reading the passages and deciding on what would be appropriate to photocopy and take back to the classroom to work on as a Readers Theatre piece. We took a transcript back to the school and then worked on the material as a class.

The students then performed the piece in role as the original trustees of the Toronto board. As they read about the importance of public education in the original board room, the audience was taken back to what was said with such dedication and generosity of spirit 150 years earlier. It was a seamless transition for the board chair David Moll to take over from the student in role as John Gooderham, the first chair of the board, and speak in the present about the same issues and concerns.

6. Art Talks Back

When we take students on field trips, we want them to get as much out of the experience as they can so that they can savor the parts that need their attention. I always think that the work done before the trip is like flipping through a magazine before reading the interesting parts. The preview is crucial for the success of the trip. Kids will be interested if they can connect what they are seeing and experiencing with what they have already learned about the topic, theme, play, or artist. They will notice far more if they have been well prepared.

For instance, if you plan to take students to the art gallery, it is important that they are prepared for what they are going to see. Be sure to teach them about the artists and the exhibit ahead of time. They need to have seen ways in which artists play with color, line, and form. They need to be intent on noticing things and to be encouraged to document their new "eyes" in a way that is comfortable for them.

Journal Responses: I recommend asking students to take a journal with them to the art gallery. I ask them to find people, feelings, and characteristics in the art that they are viewing and write down the name of the artist and picture. They may make notes in the page margins and talk to others in the class about what they are seeing and experiencing. They might also want to sketch. Leave the task as open-ended as you can.

Find the Painting: You might ask students to look at paintings with a view to finding some that match the descriptions on the next page:

- the painting with the saddest person
- the painting with the tallest mountain
- the painting with the scariest scene
- a painting with an animal
- the painting where people seem about to speak
- the painting with the best sky
- the painting with the most color
- the painting with the least color
- the most realistic painting
- the most abstract painting
- the painting with the most movement
- the painting with the most stillness
- the painting showing the most love
- the painting showing the most hate
- the painting with the most flowers
- the painting with the most blood
- the painting with the most snow
- the painting that made you feel insignificant
- the painting that made you feel guilty
- the painting that made you feel majestic
- the painting that struck you as cold
- the painting that struck you as warm
- the most confusing painting
- the most annoying painting
- the painting that brought you the most joy

If Art Could Speak: You could give each student some Art Talk Back cards and ask them to make quick comments about what they are seeing. "If art could speak, what would she say to you, the viewer?" A sample card appears below.

ART TALK BACK SHEET

What I notice about art...

_____

_____

_____

What art would say if she could explain herself to me...

_____

_____

_____

What do I do *about the kid who speaks English as a second language and needs to find other means of communication?*

7. Moving in Response to Symbols

Glenys McQueen Fuentes, a theatre professor at Brock University, has inspired me to use hieroglyphics in my teaching. Students create a myth, story, or message based on their interpretation of a series of symbols—the hieroglyphics. They work in groups of three to five to create this myth, story, or message by arranging their symbols in an order that makes sense to them. They then use those symbols as the basis for a movement exploration. The picture book *Encounter* by Jane Yolen provides excellent source material. A typical set of symbols is shown below.

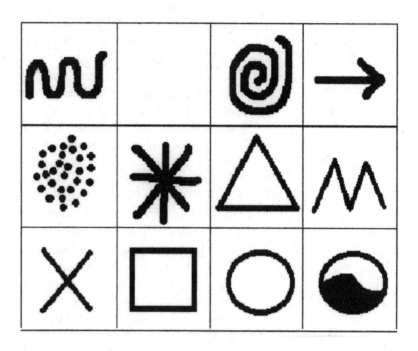

You might choose a myth, such as the Aztec myth about Quetzalcoatl. Ask students to shut their eyes and listen to the material a couple of times. Next, have a discussion centred on these questions:

- Who are these people?
- Where did they live?
- How long ago?
- What was important to them?
- How do we know that?

Give a package of six symbol cards, face down, to each small group. Explain that the group must record and preserve their myth, story, or event, but has only the symbols on the cards to work with. Advise them that where and how they leave the pattern is an important part of the message. Set a time limit of no more than ten minutes.

Tell the students that a crisis has arisen. In character as tribe members, each group must leave their lands and their record of a myth or event behind. Ask each group to move to the next group's symbol pattern. It will, of course, be different from their original. Tell them that hundreds of years have passed and that they are descendants of the people who first created the pattern. Their job is to decipher the myth, see what was important, what was emphasized, and what was left out.

Once, when Glenys McQueen Fuentes was using the hieroglyphics strategy at a culturally diverse Toronto school, a group of boys balked at moving on. As

Glenys put it, "They were clearly anxious and were unwilling to leave their message behind. When urged to do so, their anxiety level rose considerably and they simply could not contain themselves (they had been asked to move in silence). They literally blurted out, 'But what if the next group ruins our message? What if they don't see it? What if they don't understand?...'

"My recollection was that we stopped everyone for a moment and let the group of boys return to their original pattern, so they could warn their 'descendants' about where the message was and why it was so important to be extremely careful with it. At that point, we understood their worry. With *great* pride, they showed us that they had placed their message *very* carefully under a desk, in a corner of the room. The location had been chosen 'to keep the message safe from weather and people who, not recognizing its significance, might wreck, alter or ruin it.' What was even more impressive was *how* they had constructed their message. As the half file cards were in cardboard, they had created a two-storey 'house of cards' effect—with the symbols on the inside! This, too, had been done to assure it would be hidden and that there would be less chance of random violence against it. It was absolutely amazing—no wonder they were worried about it. The logic, ingenuity, thought processes, care and skill which they put into it was extraordinary, and very clear...

"The other groups each began to talk of the time and energy they had taken with their messages. Several students in other groups confessed to also worrying that the next group would might mess up their work, or not understand what they had said, or ruin their very important message.... This jumped into a conversation about how important it is that our 'messages' be understood and how difficult it was when we were misunderstood, how easy that is, compared to the difficulty of 'creating' a message. It went seamlessly into talk of perceptions, misconceptions, being 'different,' being in new lands and in new cultures and languages, of how we do not see the richness of things left behind, and no one else may understand that. It also became a discussion on how important it is to reflect on what others are trying to 'say,' on how we may only see part of the message, on being careful of and understanding of others, who are having difficulty being 'heard' or understood. I think it was by far the most extraordinary experience with the hieroglyphics that I've had—before or after."

Typically, when a group comes to a new pattern, members rework the myth through the choreography and all of them should take part in transforming the hieroglyphics into movement patterns—there should be no bystanders. The movement patterns will serve as a ritual re-enactment of the original event, which the group can present to the rest of the class.

Once all groups have presented their re-creations, perhaps with musical accompaniment, have them explain their interpretations. First, have them talk about how they interpreted the "found" pattern and finally, ask them to explain their original patternings. They could conclude the activity by making a personal reflection on what they learned, perhaps through a journal, poem, or art piece.

8. The Shirt Off Their Backs

One way to extend character study is to give students the shirt off a character's back to work with. In one instance, when I was working with Grade 7/8 students exploring the novel *Slake's Limbo* by Felice Holman, I gave each group of students a shirt. I asked them to think what they could attach to this shirt that would tell us about Slake's character. The students brought in materials and attached them to the shirt—newspaper clippings, a torn letter to Slake's mum, a subway transfer, a broken heart, a family photograph ripped in two, and more. The activity was such a success that the teachers in the school decided to adopt it with study of other novels and even with historical personages. At the end of the school year, I was invited to the library where shirts, jackets, hats, and other decorated costumes were put on display. I saw explorer Jacques Cartier's woollen scarf and a jacket worn by Métis leader Louis Riel, as well as other items representing fictional characters from picture books and novels. Students had found a way to display their art and had written character summaries. Observers were encouraged to ask questions about the items. The students defended their artistic choices and told their audience more about the characters. It was a wonderful afternoon!

9. Assuming a Dramatic Role

What do I do
about the kid who feels
insecure about writing?

Often, students do not write because they feel incapable of doing so. The irony is that the only way that they can learn how to write better is to write and learn about writing as they do so. However, when students become involved in an imaginary situation by taking on dramatic roles, we often discover that they find different and more secure voices, whether they are writing or speaking. In providing opportunities for them to take dramatic roles, we acknowledge that students have uneven experiences of the world. Their roles allow them to speak and conduct themselves in ways outside of situations that they have been in. Drama often allows students to find ways to write that have impact on them as writers and therefore move them beyond feeling to heightened understanding of human situations. Writing in role allows students' imaginations to play on what they have perceived.

There are many ways for students to write in role. Here are several that I use in my teaching.

As the storyteller: Students write a story in a role related to the work that they are doing in the classroom. For example:

*I am an elder in the village. I am going to record the story of how Lucia first came to the village and how the villagers reacted to her magical powers. (*From *The Woman Who Outshone the Sun)*

As the keeper of memories: Students keep secret diary accounts of characters' memories so that the experiences won't be forgotten. For example:

*I am Hana's suitcase and I have memories of who she was and what her life was like before she was taken away. (*From *Hana's Suitcase)*

As the person in the middle of a crisis: Students record what they have experienced "in the moment" and write initial feelings and thoughts. For example:

*I am the young boy. I have had dreams all night about what might happen to us unless we act now and get rid of these strangers who have come to our island. No one is listening to me, but I must find a way to make them hear what I have to say. (*From *Encounter)*

As the person who has to make a decision: Students write about what they are experiencing as they make a difficult decision that will change someone's life or their own situation. For example:

*I am Palmer. I am going to take the pigeon away tomorrow night. I have it all planned. If I don't act now he is sure to be a part of the pigeon shoot. (*From *Wringer)*

As the reporter: Students record the facts. For example:

*I am one of the sailors on board ship. We are going to record what we saw on the island in the logbook. (*From *The Wretched Stone)*

As the witness to an incident: Students write a "bird's eye view" account of what they see from a distance. For example:

*I am a neighbor. I see the emergency crews screeching to a halt outside the neighbor's house next door. The sound that the sirens make is terrifying and my dog begins to bark fiercely. I do not know the people who live there. I know that the parents work because I see a babysitter take the baby out for a walk during the day, but I really don't know anything about the family. (*From *Silent to the Bone)*

As the listener: After listening to confessions or arguments, students write reports. For example:

*I am Brat's imaginary friend whom she turns to when life becomes difficult. I listen and record her sadness and frustration about the bullying that is happening in her life. (*From *The Midwife's Apprentice)*

Students can write in role in different genres: diaries, reports, e-mails, letters, stories, postcards, logbook entries, journals, advertisements, "wanted" posters, biographies, and more. Their audience can be as varied as the stories that they are exploring. For example, they might write to elders, judges, parents, community members, teachers, or friends.

In one instance, I worked with a Grade 6 class that was reading Lois Lowry's *The Giver.* Their teacher had noticed that they were not taking many risks in their writing about the book. They were so used to answering questions and summarizing chapters that they found it difficult to write about their thoughts and opinions in a critical way. The teacher invited me into his classroom to work with the students and do some writing in role. He wanted to find a way for the students to look at one of the novel's themes—obedience at all costs— and allow their imaginations to help them understand what that means.

Recognizing How Role Affects Writing: In my first session, I met the students and found out what they were thinking about the novel. They were at different parts of the book, but all had read about the concept of being released from the community because you were too old, disobedient, or defective in some way. When I asked them what they thought about the idea, they did not have many opinions. The students knew book details, but did not seem to be connected to the material in any emotional way.

The next session was very different. I went early to the school and set up the classroom so that the students were working in groups of five. The tables and desks were cleared and underneath one chair in each group, I taped this message:

Your are a fine, upstanding member of the community. You obey the laws, work hard, and contribute significantly to the life of the place. Unfortunately, you have an 11-year-old daughter who has been misbehaving. She has not done anything too bad yet, but you are worried that if she continues to disobey the laws, people will begin to find out and talk, and the authorities will make the decision that she will have to be "released" from the community. You have come to a conference to meet members of a support group that have been instructed to get you to tell your story. They will ask you questions that might be difficult for you to answer, but you must try to do the best you can. You do not want to lose your daughter, but you know that you are not allowed to lie.

Once the students entered the classroom and went to their desks, I asked them to check under their chairs to see if a sheet was attached. If there was, they were to take their chair and go out into the hall, where they could read the missive with the other people who had received it. They could talk quietly about how they were going to handle the questions they expected to face.

Meanwhile, the remaining students became committees of people who had to ask the hard questions. Each group received a sheet with this information:

You are members of a support group who are "helping" people who have family members in danger of being released from the community because they are disobedient in some way. The person that you are about to meet is a fine, upstanding member of the community. This person obeys the laws, works hard and contributes significantly to the life of the place. Unfortunately, he/she has an 11-year-old daughter who has been misbehaving. The daughter has not done anything too bad yet, but you are worried that if she continues to disobey the laws, the authorities will make the decision that she will have to be "released" from the community. As members of the support group, you are required to get this person to talk about the situation and you must give instructions about what must be done to "control" the 11-year-old girl. Talk briefly as committee members about how you will set up the support group to get the parent to talk. How will you get the story and what questions will you ask? What will you do or say to get the truth?

The students out in the hall entered in role and the interviews got under way. Then I stopped the sessions and asked for silence. I gave all the students a card each and asked them to write in role. I asked the parents to write a diary account about what they were experiencing in the support group. The diary, of course, was something that was not allowed, but they kept one anyway and made sure that it remained hidden. I provided these questions as prompts:

- Did you answer the questions about your daughter as truthfully as you could?
- What pressures did you feel?
- What questions were swimming around in your mind as you were being interviewed?
- How much information did you feel compelled to tell?
- How uncomfortable was the interview?

Then, I asked the committee members to write a report that they would have to submit to the authorities about this case. They considered these questions:

- What were some of the questions you asked?
- What kind of reaction did you get from the parent?
- What suspicions do you have?
- What struck you as odd about this person's demeanor?
- What recommendation would you make to the authorities to control this situation?

The students wrote in role and then shared their writing in an Inner/Outer Circle formation (see pages 60–61). I juxtaposed the writing of the committee members, which was cold and detached, with the emotional writing of the parents. The students were riveted by the experience and spent the rest of the class talking about the role that control plays in the book. They then began to talk about what kinds of restraints they experienced in their own lives.

Here is some of the writing that resulted from the class.

Mother

I know that I have to be extra careful writing in this diary. Personal writing of any kind is forbidden. (Actually, I keep the diary hidden under my mattress. This is the one disobedience that I allow myself.) I have just met with the "Committee of Adjustment and Safety" as they called themselves. Apparently, they have been spying on my family for over a year now and they have some concerns about my daughter, Jackie, who has been sneaking out at night to look at the stars. I did not know that this was happening. They said that they did not believe me and have ordered me to put a lock on her bedroom door. They say that if this happens again she might be released. I don't want this to happen. We might not be an emotional family, but we are a close one. I am very frightened. I will speak to Jackie at supper tonight and find out what has been going on.

Committee member

Met today with Rachel, mother of an 11-year-old girl who has been seen sneaking out of her bedroom at night to do forbidden things. The mother said that she is unaware of the situation, but we did not believe her. We also know that she (the mother) keeps a diary under her bed and the committee will be speaking to her about that at our next meeting. The mother pretended to be surprised about her daughter's behavior, but we know better. There might be more than one person being released from that family in the next few days!

10. Using Strategies That Lead to Log Writing

What do I do
about the kid who really
doesn't want to write?

Usually the incidents that happen on a boat are put in a logbook. The sentences are short and to the point because there is not much time to write. Also, if there is a storm, the entry has to be made quickly. In other words, the form of writing is focused and not too intimidating. In my work with one Grade 4 class, where there were many students who did not like to write, I chose Chris Van Allsburg's *The Wretched Stone*, a story about a crew of sailors who discover an uncharted island. In order to get as far as the logbook writing, I had to employ several other strategies first.

To engage student attention, I had the class break into pairs. Each partner received a map of the area in which they lived, but one of the two maps was missing ten items. The partners had to work together to find the missing towns, roads, symbols, lakes, and island. I then asked them to imagine that places could actually disappear. What would that be like? We had a long discussion as we imagined driving towards the nearest town and suddenly not being able to find it. We then talked about how maps change as countries change. Many of the students had not realized that maps record the present and change as the world changes.

I wrote a quotation, "Life aboard a clipper was brutal and rewards were few," on the board to reinforce the idea of a hard life on the high seas. We then looked at the picture of the ship on the picture book's cover and I asked students to make predictions about the story and tell me what they thought sailors do, think about, and feel most of the time.

Next, we brainstormed what crew members would have to do to keep the ship in "shipshape" condition. Roles included mending the sails, reading the maps, mooring the ship, and keeping the log record. I asked students to imagine that they were doing some sort of work on the ship. When I touched students on the shoulder, they were to freeze in character and answer my questions about their work and travels. After a discussion about the role of log maker, I read the book to the moment that the sailors decide to go to the mysterious island and investigate what is there.

I went into role as the captain's first mate (see pages 38–39) and said,

"I have been asked by the Captain to take the crew ashore to get fresh water and fruit. I am more than a little worried about going ashore. Something is odd. This island is not on the map. The Captain scoffs at my worries and says that I must obey orders. I have agreed to go only if we are all allowed to take our logbooks and record what we see. I have insisted that when we get ashore we split up and stay in small groups. You have only one hour to get what you need and to be back as a whole crew so that we can row back to the ship. You will not have a lot of time to get food and water but you will be observing as you go and you might see things that are unusual. Please take time with your partner to record what you see. Remember to date your work and keep your logbook with you at all times. If you see something unusual I would prefer that you leave it where it is but make sure to describe it in detail in your log."

Before they worked in small groups, I read the next two pages of the book. Then I asked them to imagine what they saw on the island. As it turned out, they had trouble imagining and describing what they saw, so I asked them to leave their logbooks and in their groups create tableaux. (See pages 44–46 for an outline of the "cut to…" strategy.) Finally, after every group had presented their frozen images of the island, I asked them to return to their logbooks and record what they saw. I also provided them with a rubric to guide their writing, and the classroom teacher and I worked with each group to help them develop something that the Captain would find interesting to read. A few logbook entries are show below. The first is the draft and the second the result of the work with the rubric.

> *May 23, 1843*
> *We have found a cave with bones and gold on this mysterious island. We are hungry and thirsty. We haven't eaten in 3 days. These are our final words for our log.*

> *May 23, 1843*
> *We have found a cave with bones and gold on this mysterious island. We are hungry and thirsty. We haven't eaten in 3 days. We are planning to bring back samples to show to the Captain. The gold is very beautiful with jewels embedded in it. It is very heavy and we have to share carrying it with us because it makes us very tired. The bones are very large and seem to be from a human. Who used to live here? This is all we can manage to write because we are very weak. These are our final words for our log.*

Besides the value of logbook writing, the exercise reminded me that sometimes students need to visualize material before they write and work with it in some physical way. Also, the work with the rubric (see the sample below) elicited writing that was far better than first drafted.

Ideas

❏ Was our log entry clear?
❏ Did we put down enough information?

Organization

❏ Did we begin our log entry with the date?
❏ Did we tell what really happened?
❏ Did we record the important information?

Voice

❏ Does the journal entry sound as if it could have been written by the sailor on the ship?
❏ Will the reader of the entry be interested in what is happening?

Word choice

❏ Have we used new words that we have learned as sailors?
❏ Have we used words that we love?
❏ Have we used words that would make the reader believe that we are sailors?

Mechanics

❏ Have we used sentences?
❏ Did we leave spaces between the words?
❏ Did we use capital letters correctly?
❏ Did we do our best on spelling?
❏ Did we get someone else to read this and respond?

The challenging part of teaching is leaving an impression on students so that they become more thoughtful, imaginative, knowledgeable, critical, aware, and kind. Teaching needs to challenge students to keep on asking the difficult questions—the ones that have many answers. Learning in classrooms needs to be about the big things in life: relationships that are complex, problems that do not have easy solutions, ambiguous meanings, and perceptions that demand to be altered again and again. We need to teach our students to pay attention to details and to be open to new ways of thinking about their lives and the world in which they live.

CHAPTER 5

Evaluating and Assessing the Learning

Good assessment always begins with a vision of success.
Richard J. Stiggins

Assessment and evaluation are the responsibilities of every teacher. Assessment happens daily, informs our practice, and helps us figure out what our students are understanding and learning as we teach. We listen to their questions and answers, watch them work in groups, hear their reading, respond to what they have written, observe them find ways to represent what they want to say through the arts, and record our impressions of the way in which they have achieved their goals. We gather information and track our students' progress in a variety of ways. We scrutinize the work that is presented to us and identify students' strengths and needs. We reflect on how they are doing. This reflection informs our practice and allows us to determine how activities and events in the classroom could be restructured so that all students are successful in learning the material presented to them.

Evaluation is the process of judging the worth of student work. It should be based on data gathered through assessment using established criteria. Kids need to learn before they are judged. You shouldn't give a mark for an oral report unless they have been taught how to speak in public and have been given many different opportunities to do so. You shouldn't "take marks off for grammar and spelling" unless you have taught them those concepts and given them lots of practice and feedback. Also, you can't give marks for group work in good conscience unless you have taught the group process skills necessary for the successful achievement of group goals. Indeed, you should not give out marks until everyone has been taught the skills, has had time to practise them in a context that makes sense, and understands how they are being judged so that they can perform to those criteria.

For some students the way in which they are "marked" is a mystery to them. Be sure to demystify the experience and make assessment and evaluation clear. Students need to feel that you are going to give them time, space, resources, and practice to learn and that when it comes time to evaluate their work, you will do it fairly.

Assessment as a Dynamic Process

There are three main types of assessment: diagnostic, formative, and summative. *Diagnostic* assessment examines the prior knowledge and skills that a student has. Because of that, it does not result in a mark or grade that "counts" and is useful for the teacher in adjusting the course or program. *Formative* assessment can result in a mark or grade, but for feedback purposes only. It gives useful, meaningful feedback to students to improve their knowledge and skills, and requires student input and response. Finally, summative assessment requires demonstrated achievement of specific criteria linked to ministry of education expectations. It determines what students have achieved by the end of a unit, term, or school year and results in a grade or mark.

Various ways of assessing are outlined below.

Anecdotal records: These include observation guides of students' growth and behavior, notes about reading, writing, artwork, and so on, observations of participation in role-playing, reports about interviews, either formal or informal, inventories, and self-assessments.

Tracking records: Forms of such records include checklists that record student effort and participation, videotapes, audio tapes, photographs, surveys, responses to questions, and questionnaires.

Demonstrations of process: These include drafts of written work in writing folders, self-assessments, peer assessments of group participation, journals, conferences, graphic organizers, and teacher-student conferences.

Products: These encompass completed worksheets, writing in role, artwork, research reports, diagrams, debates, and tests. Remember, though, that not every task needs to be graded.

Assessment should not be seen as something that is linear and final. Think of it as a wheel that is turning, gathering information to inform practice, empowering us all to reach new understandings. As we gather our assessment data, we should be using it to inform the way that we teach. Let's say that you ask students to do a performance task and, as they are doing it, you see that they have missed key understandings. You realize that for many of them the concepts are still too difficult and you will have to go back and find a way to help them gain a better understanding of the material. You do not have to make this task "count." Assessment data should keep us asking questions and refining our program and teaching so that more students can learn successfully.

1. Keeping Anecdotal Records

Anecdotal records typically focus on student learning skills and behavior. You can consider characteristics such as these when assessing an individual student over time:

❏ Explains things to others   ❏ Takes initiative
❏ Listens to instructions   ❏ Is motivated to learn
❏ Works independently   ❏ Stays on task
❏ Works better with a partner   ❏ Is shy but involved
❏ Would benefit from working in a
 group where there is support

Questions to Ask Yourself
- How will I gather evidence that the students have learned what has been intended?
- How will I provide feedback to the students?
- How will I support students who need more time or a different approach?
- What can I say or do to make everyone feel that the time has been well spent?

Here are some questions you might ask yourself as you teach and assess.

- Are students interested in the material that I am presenting?
- Have I created bridges of understanding?
- Have I personally acknowledged everyone in the class this week in a positive way?
- Have I modelled the way that I want students to write? talk? interact?
- Have I had students respond in a personal way to what is going on in the classroom?
- Am I aware of how students are interacting socially with one another and have I helped them address any issues of concern?
- Have I encouraged them to revise their work or have I been too product-oriented and rushed them to get to the product?
- Have I planned activities that will engage the students in ways that will connect them to the material and to one another?
- What programming changes can I make so that all will benefit?

2. Interviewing to Prompt Reflection

As I indicated in the first chapter, interviews are an effective way to get to know your students at the beginning of the year. They also serve as an essential way to assess what your students are learning in the classroom. They provide you with an opportunity to find out in more depth what the students are perceiving and learning, and allow you to rethink your program's goals and activities.

Interviews in Character: Sometimes I ask students to interview main characters in the novel that we are studying or historical personages that we are reading about. The interviewer asks the character questions like these:

- How does it feel to be famous?
- What did you contribute to what happened?
- What do you think is the scene that you will be remembered for? Describe the scene for me.
- What do you hope people will say about your character in the years to come?
- What do you think makes you so interesting to people?
- What are you going to do now that the book is finished, published, and read?

The value of this assessment strategy is that it allows the interviewer or teacher to find out how much information the student has learned and what kind of critical thinking processes he or she can engage in.

When interview responses to questions such as "How did you hear about the voyage?" are recorded on a chart, the creative activity can take the place of a test or quiz.

Teacher-Student Interviews: You can set up times to talk with your students one-to-one. You might ask questions on these topics.

- Classroom work
  What is the biggest challenge facing you at the moment?

Which of these activities do you feel comfortable doing?
For which ones will you need support?
What is your biggest distraction? How can we limit the distractions so that you can get your work done?

- Homework
  What problems are you encountering as you try to do your homework? Space? Time? Support? Level of difficulty? Resources?
  What kind of homework plan can we put in place to make you accountable to yourself? to others?

- Peer pressure
  What kind of role are you playing in group situations?
  What do you do when you find that you are dominating the discussion? OR How can you contribute more to the group discussion?
  What do you do when you get locked into your own position in group discussions and have trouble listening to others' ideas?
  How can you find a way to get the other students to listen to what you have to say?

- Learning strategies
  Let's look at all of the different ways that you can tap into learning. Let's make a plan about how we can achieve more in each of these areas: reading, writing, speaking, listening.

- Life goals
  What kinds of personal goals do you want to achieve?
  What kinds of challenges do you think you want to pursue?

Beyond personal interviews, you could ask students to respond to prompts about themselves as students now and in the future. They could respond either before or after their interviews, and their ideas could be discussed and acted upon. A list of prompts appear on the next page.

Before an interview, you will probably have a good idea that a student would benefit from using various organizational strategies. You might offer this summary of strategies that should help the student learn.

❏ List all of your ideas.
❏ Read your writing out loud.
❏ Jot down concepts.
❏ Draw or sketch your ideas.
❏ Organize information into categories.
❏ Make some sort of visual pattern to help you see the connections.
❏ Prioritize what you need to do.
❏ Keep a calendar and refer to it daily.
❏ Record what you need to remember to do for homework and what you have agreed to bring to school for the next day.
❏ Ask your friends to remind you of what you need to do.
❏ Use the Login centre to make an appointment with the teacher to have some ideas clarified.
❏ Use a tape recorder to record your initial ideas for the project.

What do I do
about the kid who is disorganized when it comes to learning?

Prompts to Reflection

The best thing about me as a student:

_____

_____

What I know about the way in which I learn:

_____

_____

What I am happiest learning about in school:

_____

_____

How I react when I am faced with a difficult task:

_____

_____

How I react when I am in a group that is not working cooperatively:

_____

_____

What you would be surprised to discover that I am really good at:

_____

_____

Things that, as a student, I would like to improve on:

_____

_____

What I can do for myself:

_____

_____

What adults can do to help me:

_____

_____

What my peers can do to help me:

_____

_____

What the program can do:

_____

_____

What the teacher can do:

_____

_____

3. Using Exemplars to Establish Clear Criteria

It is helpful for students to see what you are asking for in terms of achievement. Exemplars—graded work at various levels—can be distributed or shown on an overhead to help students see what excellent, very good, good, and fair performances are. They can be drawn from work that has been done in the class, from collections that teachers have assembled over the years, or from state or provincial benchmarks of achievement.

Teachers need to exercise their best judgment when they use exemplars in their teaching. Exemplars should encourage, not discourage, and help demystify how students are graded. They can also give students something to aim for. If you include a rubric (see pages 82–83), students can see what is expected and how it is achieved.

4. Developing Student Profiles

If you take the time to record student interests, backgrounds, questions, experiences, and responses, you will gain a more complete picture of each student in your classroom. You can refer to these profiles when students are having difficulty finding something to write about or having trouble completing the tasks before them. If you understand where students are at, what kinds of things interest them, what kinds of difficulties they experience when faced with a complex task, how they react, and how they wish they could tackle the tasks to succeed at learning, you will be able to steer them into uncharted territory. They will need proper support, but this support does not always have to come from you. You could strategically place a student in a group of people who will help her achieve in areas in which she usually struggles.

Invite students to consider these matters and more: books read, projects completed, different kinds of writing done, things to be completed, ways to get all this done, people who can help, kinds of information and help needed, and a timeline for completing the work in chunks so that they are not overwhelmed. The information will provide you with more insight about how to help.

5. Providing Rehearsal Opportunities

It is important to provide many rehearsals before you grade. Give the same kind of assessment, or performance, task many times and have the students grade themselves or grade for one trait only. Ensure that they have had lots of practice working with a concept in numerous different ways before making a judgment and determining a mark.

6. Fostering Self and Peer Assessment

Students need to self-monitor their progress. They should always ask themselves: "Am I getting this? If I'm not, I need to let my teacher know that." Alternatively, they can work with a partner and get immediate feedback on something they have done.

When it comes to assessing writing, encourage students to think in these terms:

- First drafts of writing should be seen as first thoughts on a page. Students should record their thoughts in whatever shape they find easiest.
- First drafts should also be seen as something that will require revision, not just editing. It is a good idea for students to write on every other line so that they will have room to add new ideas when they go back to revise.
- Students can clarify meaning by expanding, rejecting, and reshaping. They can use highlighters, pencils, and scissors, and rework the work!
- Students should work on the mechanics as they are doing the rethinking. They may find it a good idea to read what they have written out loud. That will often tell them what they have to do to make the meaning clearer.
- Reading writing to a partner is worthwhile. Students can listen to the partner's opinions and then go back to reshape the work. Feedback is essential for writers and can improve the work.
- Advise students to keep all drafts of their work. Material that they have cut might be good to use when they write again.

7. Using Journals for Assessment

Journals can serve as valid assessment tools. Have students keep a checklist in the front or back of their journals and at different times, get them to focus in on one of the following:

- ideas that the student has never thought of before
- ideas that the student would like to pursue
- spelling
- best sentences
- amazing quotes
- beautiful pictures
- new vocabulary
- writing
- summarizing
- thinking
- questioning
- books read or books that the student wants to read
- Web sites that have provided helpful new information
- new ways of knowing

Ask students to look through their journals periodically and have them assess their strengths and weaknesses. Can they see how their writing, thinking, and forms of response are changing over the course of the year? Do they know what they still need to work on? When you arrange interviews with students, ask them to bring their journals and assess themselves for strengths and weaknesses beforehand. You can then make a plan to address any concerns together.

You might remind students that everyone experiences the writing process and that it takes a long time to produce pieces of writing. Commitment to the writing, an audience that cares, lots of time to think, and people who will give constructive feedback are all part of the process. Journal writing can play an important role in the development of finished work. A summary of the steps leading to sharing and publishing appears as an appendix. You might offer it to students as a way to analyze and break down the task of writing into more accessible chunks.

What do I do
about the kid who gets
badly discouraged about
writing?

My Journal

Trends that I have observed

- ❏ My writing is getting clearer.
- ❏ I am writing more.
- ❏ I am becoming more adventurous in my writing.
- ❏ I am paying more attention to detail.
- ❏ I am aware of some of the strategies that are helping me write.
- ❏ My reading is becoming more fluent.
- ❏ I am reading more.

- ❏ I am reading different kinds of texts.
- ❏ I am talking about what I am reading.
- ❏ I am encouraging others to read what I have read.
- ❏ I am always on the lookout for more to read.
- ❏ I am aware of some of the strategies that are helping me read.

I am becoming aware of how I learn.

- ❏ I find that if I can make pictures in my head, I _____
- ❏ I find that if I can talk about information before I write, I _____

- ❏ I find that if I wonder aloud first, then _____
- ❏ I find it most difficult to concentrate and stay on task when _____

I am becoming more confident as I work in groups.

- ❏ I am trying on different roles in group situations.
- ❏ If I disagree I am able to tell people why.
- ❏ I am learning not to interrupt.

- ❏ I am trying to be patient.
- ❏ I work hard to stay on topic.
- ❏ I am learning how to be diplomatic.

I am connecting my learning to

- ❏ other things we are learning in class
- ❏ things that I knew before

- ❏ questions that I am writing down
- ❏ What I am experiencing in my life

I am remembering to

- ❏ date all of my work
- ❏ hand in my homework
- ❏ ask if I do not understand
- ❏ seek help from dictionaries, a thesaurus, my friends, teachers, and others

- ❏ watch the way that I interact with others
- ❏ notice people, events, and things that are happening around me

I still struggle with _____

Sometimes I get stuck on _____

I am determined to _____

I know that I can rely on _____

I still want to _____

8. Creating Rubrics

Traditionally, we have left the student out of the process of evaluation. A rubric allows everyone—teacher, students, and parent/guardian—to know the expectations for a project or assignment. There are no surprises and everyone is aware of the specific criteria pertaining to how to get a good mark. Teachers can design the rubric with their students. It is often a good idea to ask for student feedback and to revise the rubric in the light of what they say.

Here is the process I go through with my students when I create a rubric.

After introducing the task that will be evaluated, I specify what I will be looking for in terms of what students will be learning, for example, understanding the concepts; being critically aware of various interpretations; being able to communicate what is being learned. Then I say to my students:

"What will it look like, sound like, and read like if you are achieving really well in one of these categories?" We then describe the criteria for achievement at the different levels. An example using three criteria, or "look fors," is outlined below.

Level 4

demonstrating a thorough understanding of _____

"When I listen to your conversation, I am hearing you use lots of vocabulary that we have talked about in class."

being critically aware of various interpretations

"I hear you discussing the ideas that were presented in the reading from various points of view. You are using such phrases as 'on the other hand,' 'it could be,' 'I wonder,' and 'I can see this a little differently because.' I can see by the questions that you have handed in that you are really thinking beyond what we have been talking about and are wanting to get more information."

being able to communicate what is being learned

"When you present your information, you are very articulate and confident. You write with a clear purpose and are aware of your audience."

Level 3

demonstrating an understanding of _____

"When I listen to your conversation, I hear you use some of the vocabulary that we have talked about in class."

being critically aware of various interpretations

"I hear you discussing a lot of the ideas that were presented in the reading from your own point of view. I can see by the questions that you have handed in that you are beginning to think about what you are learning and to make some connections."

being able to communicate what is being learned

"When you present your information, you are articulate and confident. You write with a purpose and are aware of your audience."

Level 2

demonstrating a limited understanding of _____

"When I listen to your conversation, I hear you use at least one new word that we have talked about in class."

being critically aware of various interpretations
"I hear you discussing a few of the ideas that were presented in the reading from your own point of view. I can see by the questions that you have handed in that you need to get some more information so that you can begin to make some connections."
being able to communicate what is being learned
"When you present your information, you are becoming more articulate and confident. You write with a purpose, but you need to be more aware of your audience."

Level 1

demonstrating little evidence of an understanding of _____
"When I listen to your conversation, I notice that you are not clear about the concepts we have been learning. You need to come and see me so that we can talk about how you can get this information and succeed at the task."
being critically aware of various interpretations
"You are only thinking about this topic from one perspective and you do not seem to be aware that there might be other ways to look at this topic."
being able to communicate what is being learned
"Before you begin to communicate the information, you need to become more secure in what you know and want to say. Please come to see me so that we can find ways to help you understand the material."

9. Developing Portfolios

Portfolios are not objects. They are vehicles for ongoing assessment by students. They represent activities and processes (selecting, comparing, self-evaluation, sharing, goal setting) more than they do products.

Robert J. Tierney, Mark A. Carter, and Laura E. Desai

Portfolios are collections of work that students have done and are doing. They showcase a range of work that is in progress, finished, or has the feel of being finished. They can encompass work that students feel demonstrate tangible evidence of accomplishment as well as work that the students want to return to at a later date when they have more time, skill, and knowledge. Serving as both an assessment and evaluation tool, they can be used by teachers and students to illuminate students' strengths and give information and guidance to both students and teacher in terms of their needs, progress, and accomplishment. As they create portfolios, students learn about their own learning and become more reflective and self-aware of what they are doing when they are doing schoolwork. They see where they began and where they are at the present. They become aware of the improvements they have made.

Portfolios allow students to feel ownership. Students can see their work not as a series of assignments that need to be handed in and marked, but as a process that is engaging, informative, thoughtful, negotiable, and self-affirming for all.

Portfolios give students and teacher a series of "snapshots" about learning. Students choose the items to be included in their portfolios and then offer information about their choices, perhaps in the context of student-teacher conferencing. When students confer with teachers and others about the range and quality of work in their portfolios, they can look critically at what they have included, analyze the offerings, and then set new goals for their learning. On the other hand, you can use portfolios to examine the effort that the students are expending, to make plans for improvement or change of direction, to look at the process in use and find other strategies that might be more useful and effective, and to make judgments about student achievement.

Be sure to provide guidance and time for students to compare and select pieces for their portfolios. Spend time with the whole class, teaching them about what to include and how to showcase it, and write all of the ideas generated on chart paper so students can refer to them when they set out to pull their portfolios together.

See pages 85 and 86 for a student handout about portfolios and what might go into them.

Student Portfolios

What should be included in a portfolio? The items can be as varied as the curriculum and as the students who are creating the portfolios. It is important that the list of items not become prescriptive. Everyone should be open to new, fresh ideas.

You will want to custom-design your portfolio to reflect the ways that you are learning. Your portfolio will develop out of the work that you do on projects, in class, on field trips, and in other activities throughout the year.

Any of the following kinds of items may be included in your portfolio:

- sketches
- journal entries
- personal narratives
- diagrams
- poetry
- questions
- lists of topics
- self-assessments
- factual information about what you are studying
- first drafts and revisions
- notes about your reading, thinking, and imaginings
- ideas
- reading responses
- audiotaped readings
- roles on the wall
- agendas
- timelines
- memories
- dreams
- maps
- reading logs
- writing in role exercises
- personal anecdotes
- stories
- photographs
- reports
- letters
- documents
- quotes from your reading
- video clips
- tests
- comments from friends and teachers
- goals

Depending on the nature of your portfolio's contents, you might showcase the material in a folder, on computer discs with a user guide, on a video, or in other ways that you can devise.

When it comes time to develop your portfolio, be sure to do the following:

❏ Collect all of your work.

❏ Look at the variety.

❏ Note strengths and areas that need improvement.

❏ See the effort that you have expended.

❏ Assess each piece and think about why you might want to include it in your portfolio.

❏ Use stickies to make comments about the work.

❏ Talk to others—teacher, parent, friend, classmate, older student—about your portfolio and listen to their suggestions.

❏ Revise your portfolio with these questions in mind:
  • Does my portfolio show a variety of work?
  • Does it give a snapshot of how I have improved?
  • Does it indicate what I have been thinking about? responding to?
  • Does it give me and others an idea of where I have come from and where I would like to go?
  • Does it represent who I am as a learner?

❏ Remember to date all your work.

❏ Revise your goals.

❏ "Own" your work and be proud of how special you are.

❏ Be aware of how much you have learned!

10. Designing a Culminating Task

A culminating task allows students to create and present the largest, richest piece of work in a unit. All other work and learnings prepare students to do this task. When teachers design culminating tasks, they generally "design down," that is, they begin with the learning at the end in mind.

As you design a culminating task, it is a good idea to ask yourself these questions:

- Will the students be interested in the task?
- Does the task simulate real-world situations? (a board game, the sports section from the newspaper, film footage with soundtrack, an art exhibition with detailed accounts of the artists, a poetry café)
- Do the sub-tasks that I have designed lead up to the culminating task?
- Have I taught my students everything that I am expecting them to demonstrate in the culminating task?
- Will they be propelled into demonstrating the knowledge and skills that I have taught them in the sub-tasks of the unit?
- Will the students have options and choices as they complete the task?
- Will the task encourage students to rethink, apply, expand on concepts, and explain and justify their understandings?
- Have I made the task complex enough so that multiple steps must be taken to complete it?
- Have I given students enough time so that they can successfully complete the task?
- Have I clearly and concisely described the multiple steps in the task?
- Do the students know the criteria by which their performance or product will be judged?

A wide variety of culminating tasks are identified on page 88.

So the culminating task governs the development of your unit. When planning your unit, be sure to make use of a template (see the appendix on page 104 for an example) and a calendar with all the school activities. As Richard Courtney has said, "The map is not the territory." Keep in mind that the unit you are planning will be changed and modified as you work with your students, listen to their questions, understand their different needs, and set new challenges for them that you did not think of earlier. Students learn best when moderate challenges are presented to them at various strategic stages in the learning process. Give students an idea of where they are headed.

Integration as a way to approach curriculum from many angles

Tasks that allow students to draw on various aspects of their separate subject learning and synthesize their experiences encourage students to learn in different ways from different angles.

Curriculum needs to be approached from many angles. As a parallel, consider sculpture. When I go to a sculpture gallery, I take my time looking at the individual sculptures from a variety of perspectives. I walk around a piece of work and look at the ways that the light plays on it. I see different things from different angles and gain a new understanding about the piece. I am affected differently by each new looking. Classrooms need to be places where students

A human being is made to synthesize all forms of experience into one harmonious functioning whole. If experience is too incoherent to integrate, we may mentally or physically negate what we can't assimilate...

James Moffett and Betty Jane Wagner

Culminating Tasks

Create a museum. (See pages 91–93.)

Prepare and present a documentary scene.

Prepare and present an anthology.

Research, investigate, and perform a trial.

Prepare a poetry café, in which students choose poems to present to an audience in different ways, including solo reading, choral reading, and Readers Theatre.

Prepare a slide show of tableaux with voice over.

Design a gallery of artwork complete with artist statements and guided tours.

Prepare and engage in a debate.

Compose a collage of famous speeches and bring it to life.

Design a scavenger hunt complete with clues, maps, instructions, incentives, and prizes.

Design a memorial to famous men and women in history or a memorial to characters in books.

Design a futuristic science fair.

Design a Web page.

Prepare for a camping trip.

Design a brochure that includes research, a biography, pictures, and photographs.

Research letters written by historical personages and present them as Readers Theatre.

Create advertisements for travel back to a certain historical period.

Create commercials for radio and TV, encouraging novel reading.

Design a series of billboards to encourage drivers to go home and read novels.

Create a magazine with articles, ads, obituaries, and music reviews.

Produce a family album.

Develop a poetry anthology with pictures.

Write a guidebook to the world of the novel.

Develop a portfolio.

Design a game board complete with instructions, play pieces, and box.

Organize a celebration

Make a book of lists.

Organize a swearing-in ceremony.

Create a tapestry or quilt, including artist statement.

Create a radio show of oral histories.

Make a PowerPoint presentation.

and their teachers are awakened to new ways of thinking and living in the world, where they see, hear, and feel in often unexpected ways.

Integration allows teachers to find authentic (not forced) ways of connecting various aspects of the curriculum. Content, knowledge, and understanding can be drawn from one discipline to enrich and apply to another. Various aspects of the students' separate subject learning can be brought into a meaningful association through planned projects that carefully and skillfully integrate curriculum areas.

Integration allows you to teach in a way that makes sense to the students. They are encouraged to see different perspectives, connect facts and figures, think critically and imaginatively about ideas, work with materials in a variety of ways, and produce oral, written, artistic, dramatic, and musical pieces in authentic, contextualized presentational forms. Integrated curriculum addresses students' multiple intelligences or learning styles and permits avenues of expression not limited to words or numbers. It also necessitates cooperation and sharing of expertise among teaching staff as they work together to determine how to teach the curriculum from various approaches.

Ten tips on planning an integrated unit

1. Don't force the connections.
2. Brainstorm all the possibilities.
3. Seek out help from your colleagues.
4. Get support from the school administration.
5. Let the parents and the community know what you are planning. Write a letter to the parents and community members asking for their help and interest.
6. Negotiate the timelines with your students so that they do not become overwhelmed by the work and enjoy the journey of learning.
7. Monitor group process at all times and intervene to help the groups work well together.
8. Keep in mind the different kinds of learning styles in your classroom. Some students are going to do really well at the research and not as well in the dramatic presentation; some are going to want to write up the report and others will want to do the artwork. The trick is to partner up people to support and teach one another along the way. Students should set learning goals and push themselves in areas that they know that they are weak in. (If the unit is working well, students should feel supported as well as challenged.)
9. Get in touch with the school librarian to obtain resources and other ideas. Book the library for several classes.
10. Start from a culminating task and map backwards.

What do I do
about the kid who needs to see the whole picture and learn in different ways?

Planning an Integrated Unit: Guiding Questions

When you and your colleagues plan an integrated unit, consider these questions together. Being able to plan with your colleagues and hear what they have to say about what they know so well is also an invaluable, if informal in-service.

- Analysis of student performance
  Let's think carefully about all the students whom we teach.
  What are the challenges?
  Have we looked at all the learning styles and intelligences?
  Who in our classes would really benefit from being involved in a unit that will tap into individual strengths and interests?

- Diagnosis of educational situations
  Let's think about what is expected in terms of standards and expectations.
  What can we design that will interest and challenge everyone?
  Who will really shine during this unit?
  What can we design that will allow students to show creativity and learn independently?

- Integration linked to expectations
  How many subjects can we integrate without forcing the connections?
  What theme or topic will be large enough and important enough for solid integration to take place?
  How can we make sure that the content can be linked to their emotional, physical, and social lives as well as their intellectual lives?

- Time
  What's feasible in terms of time?
  How can we restructure the schedule and timetable?
  How can we maintain needed routines so kids will know that there is a structure in place?

- Assessment and evaluation
  What do we want students to know and be able to do by the end of this unit?
  How will we be able to measure what they have learned?
  What kind of performance task can we design to inform us of all of this learning?
  How can we ensure that the judgments we are going to make are fair?
  What kind of culminating task can we design to inspire the students to keep working towards a learning goal that matters?

- Resources
  Where can we go to find models of integration?
  Who can we ask to help our students do the research they need to do to make this work successful?
  What kinds of human stories will engage students?
  What kinds of source material can we bring into the classroom?
  What kinds of teaching strategies can we use to help students find the meaning in the material that they are researching?
  What kinds of presentational options can we teach them so that they will be able to share their work with an audience and be successful doing so?
  Who can we call on to become a guest speaker?
  What field trips can we organize to enhance what is being learned?

- Reflecting and refining
  How can we ensure that the students will enjoy the experience and learn a great deal about what we are teaching?
  How can we organize ourselves to get feedback from staff administration and students so that the unit can be improved?
  How can we publish our results so that the work we have done can serve as a resource for others?

Nobody's Child

Alone, in the dreary, pitiless
    street,
With my torn old dress and bare
    cold feet,
All day I wandered to and fro,
Hungry and shivering and
    nowhere to go;
The night's coming on in
    darkness and dread,
And the chill sleet beating upon
    my bare head;

Oh! Why does the wind blow
    upon me so wild?
Is it because I'm nobody's child?

Oh! What shall I do when the
    night comes down
In its terrible darkness all over the
    town?
Shall I lay me down 'neath the
    angry sky,
On the cold hard pavements alone
    to die?
When the beautiful children their
    prayers have said,
And mothers have tucked them
    snugly in bed,
No dear mother ever upon me
    smiled—
Why is it, I wonder, that I'm
    nobody's child?

Phila H. Case

*If our teaching is to be an art,
we must remember that it is not
the number of good ideas that
turns our teaching into an art
but the selection, balance and
design of those ideas...*

Lucy McCormick Calkins

Culminating tasks that provide a full picture

Since the focus here is on culminating tasks, the example provided does not cover the eleven lessons leading up to them in any detail. In this instance, I was working with inner-city students who had been chosen by their principal to attend a leadership camp. The students were there to improve their literacy and social skills while exploring a historical topic. The topic was the lives of the Home children, those children that had come from the slums of industrial England in the late 1800s and early 1900s to live with Canadian families. I thought that the goal of creating a museum of Home children would provide the students with a culminating task of some significance.

Lesson strategies included many already presented in this book: unpacking the suitcase of artifacts such as a Home child would have; creating a tableau, in this case, of the "perfect" family; reading an appropriate poem, "Nobody's Child," out loud; creating another tableau in response to the poem; doing a role on the wall based on the artifacts and poem content; writing "I am from..." poems; basing tableaux on specific historical facts; having the teacher in role as a representative of the local historical society and the students as descendants of Home children; presenting a guest speaker on the theme and visiting a museum to see how displays are structured.

Once students had done all these activities, we began to set up the museum experience. We talked about what we wanted visitors to understand about the Home children, how we would engage them in the experience, and how the various groups involved in establishing the museum would communicate with one another. I then divided the students into seven groups and gave each group one of the following tasks to perform, along with a group assessment checklist.

The brochure group: You will design the brochure that visitors to the museum pick up as they enter. The brochure's purpose is to guide visitors to the various exhibits. You might decide to include a section where the visitors write their comments about what they saw and heard about the exhibits.

Assessment checklist:
❑ We have coordinated all of the information on all of the exhibits.
❑ Our language is clear.
❑ We have a main idea.
❑ We have used graphics.
❑ We have organized the material so that it is easy to follow and will guide the visitors smoothly through the museum.
❑ We have cited our references.
❑ We have an artistic cover.
❑ We have checked the mechanics of our writing.
❑ We have left space for comments and questions.

The guide group: There will be a guide at every part of the museum to introduce the display and answer any questions. Guides can be identified by their badges which say, "Ask me ANYTHING!

Assessment checklist:
❑ Our language is clear.
❑ We have a main idea.

❏ We have coordinated what we want to say.
❏ We have rehearsed our speeches and answered one another's questions.
❏ We have revised our presentation to make it clearer.
❏ We have made sure that we talked to the display case group members so that we know what they want us to say.
❏ We have left time for comments and questions.

The soundscape group: Your group will put together a soundscape of what the journey across the ocean must have sounded like to the Home children. You may use your imaginations and your research to take your audience on a journey from farewell in London, England, to arrival by train in Peterborough, Ontario.

Assessment checklist:
❏ We brainstormed all sorts of ideas.
❏ We listened to everyone's suggestions.
❏ We came up with a main idea.
❏ We structured the experience with the audience in mind.
❏ We coordinated and organized what we wanted to present so that it had a clear beginning, middle, and end.
❏ We rehearsed our soundscape and asked for feedback from an audience.
❏ We revised our presentation to make it "work."
❏ We have left time for comments and questions.

The display case group: You are to create the artifacts and the stories that will fill the cases at the entrance to the museum. Your goal is to keep the visitors to the museum riveted by what they see and hear.

Design the display cases and fill them with artifacts that you draw or make: All of the artifacts will tell different stories. Write as if you are an artifact, such as the trunk, the last letter sent from a mother, or the contract that a parent signed for Mr. Barnardo.

Assessment checklist:
❏ We brainstormed all sorts of ideas.
❏ We listened to everyone's suggestions.
❏ We came up with a list of artifacts to go into the display cases.
❏ We designed the artifacts and their placement in the cases with the audience in mind.
❏ We wrote in role and read our writing to other group members.
❏ We listened to their feedback and incorporated their suggestions into our new version.
❏ We attached the writing to the artifact.
❏ We left time for comments and questions.

The wax museum group: You will create frozen images that can speak. When a visitor points to one of you, that figure will come alive and tell the story of his or her adventures as a Home child. The stories need to be told in such a way that the visitors will stand and listen.

Assessment checklist:
❏ We brainstormed all sorts of ideas.
❏ We listened to everyone's suggestions.

❏ We came up with a main idea.
❏ We structured the experience with the audience in mind.
❏ We coordinated and organized what we wanted to present so that it had a clear beginning, middle, and end.
❏ We created our stories and asked for feedback from the group.
❏ We revised our presentation to make it "work" for the audience.
❏ We left time for comments and questions.

The drama group: You are a troupe of actors that the museum has hired to tell the stories behind the stories. Through your research, you will likely unearth poignant stories about the experiences of the Home children. Here are some prompts for your scripted scenes:

- How could you have done this?
- If you only knew...
- They never paid me a cent.
- I want to run away.
- The only person who was kind to me...
- I was one of the lucky ones.

Assessment checklist:
❏ We brainstormed all sorts of ideas.
❏ We listened to everyone's suggestions.
❏ We improvised from the first lines of the scripts.
❏ We edited and reworked the scenes so that they were short and poignant.
❏ We structured the experience with the audience in mind.
❏ We coordinated and organized what we wanted to present so that it had a clear beginning, middle, and end.
❏ We created our scenes and asked for feedback from the group.
❏ We revised our presentation to make it "work" for the audience.
❏ We left time for comments and questions.

The reading group: From your research, write in role as characters who knew these children at various times in their lives. Then you will work together in your group to weave the reading of your writing into a Readers Theatre presentation for visitors to the museum.

Assessment checklist:
❏ We brainstormed all sorts of ideas.
❏ We listened to everyone's suggestions.
❏ We researched material and incorporated some of it in our writing in role.
❏ We edited and reworked the readings so that they worked.
❏ We structured the experience with the audience in mind.
❏ We coordinated and organized what we wanted to present so that it had a clear beginning, middle, and end.
❏ We created our Readers Theatre presentation and asked for feedback from the group.
❏ We revised our presentation to make it "work" for the audience.
❏ We left time for comments and questions.

Personal Evaluation

I was

- ❏ helpful
- ❏ ready to work
- ❏ on time
- ❏ encouraging

- ❏ ready to listen and give feedback
- ❏ respectful of others' ideas
- ❏ efficient

What I loved about this project: _____

_____

_____

_____

What I would change about this project: _____

_____

_____

_____

Group Evaluation

We

- ❏ came up with an organized plan

- ❏ worked within the time frame

- ❏ used a variety of sources

- ❏ sorted information

- ❏ negotiated with one another

- ❏ completed the project

Group members: _____

_____

_____

As teachers we need to be clear about the purposes of assessment and evaluation and to question and review our practices as much as possible. We need to think of assessment as a series of teaching strategies that inform our practice and help us plan effective learning activities. Evaluation procedures and events need to be well developed, fair, and clear to everyone. They should help students feel that they can successfully complete the performance tasks that are set out.

Assessing My Personal Goals and Needs

I know that I am good at _____

_____

I want to get good at _____

_____

What I would like to contribute to the class: _____

_____

What I need from the school to achieve my goals: _____

_____

What I need from my classmates to achieve my goals: _____

_____

What I need from my teacher to achieve my goals: _____

_____

These situations in school make me worry that I am not going to be successful: _____

_____

These situations in school make me feel successful: _____

_____

When I feel that I am not going to be successful, I _____

_____

I dream of becoming _____

_____

Thinking About Something in New Ways

Topic: _____

Your teacher may tell you to answer specific questions from this list of possibilities. Be sure to write in full sentences. Wax poetic!

1. What's the most **beautiful** thing you know about _____?

   _____

   _____

   _____

2. What's the most **interesting** thing you know about _____?

   _____

   _____

   _____

3. What's the most **boring** thing you know about _____?

   _____

   _____

   _____

4. What's the most **troubling** thing you know about _____?

   _____

   _____

   _____

5. What's the most **difficult** thing you know about _____?

   _____

   _____

   _____

6. What's the most **exciting** thing you know about _____?

_____

_____

_____

7. What's the most **dangerous** thing you know about _____?

_____

_____

_____

8. What's the most **tragic** thing you know about _____?

_____

_____

_____

9. What's the most **compelling** thing you know about _____?

_____

_____

_____

10. What's the most **fascinating** thing you know about _____?

_____

_____

_____

11. What's the most **precious** thing you know about _____?

_____

_____

_____

12. What's the most **important** thing you know about _____?

_____

_____

_____

Interviews in Role: Assessment Checklist

This checklist may be used in a variety of contexts, including the Experts Tell Us game and various studies of fictional characters and historical personages.

As an interviewer, you will be expected to

- ❏ listen to others
- ❏ project yourself into a role
- ❏ maintain the role that you are playing
- ❏ build on other questions raised
- ❏ make inferences
- ❏ synthesize information
- ❏ form an opinion
- ❏ justify your opinion based on the information received
- ❏ speak in small-group discussions (where applicable)

As the candidate or character being interviewed, you will be expected to

- ❏ listen to others
- ❏ project yourself into a role
- ❏ maintain the role that you are playing
- ❏ carry on the improvisation
- ❏ answer the questions to the best of your ability
- ❏ reveal information that is pertinent to the situation
- ❏ make inferences
- ❏ speak in small-group discussions (where applicable)

Word Discoveries Worksheet

Text: _____

_____

**Unfamiliar
words**

_Guess what
they mean.
Can you find
definitions in the
dictionary?_

**Alliterative
words**

_Example: Wild and
woolly
What effect
does this type of
repetition have?_

**Old
words**

_Guess what
they mean.
Can you find
definitions in the
dictionary?_

**Repetition
of words or
syllables**

_What effect
does this have?_

Find the Painting!

Art Gallery: _____   **Date of Visit:** _____

- The painting with the saddest person _____
- The painting with the tallest mountain _____
- The painting with the scariest scene _____
- A painting with an animal _____
- The painting where people seem about to speak _____
- The painting with the best sky _____
- The painting with the most color _____
- The painting with the least color _____
- The most realistic painting _____
- The most abstract painting _____
- The painting with the most movement _____
- The painting with the most stillness _____
- The painting showing the most love _____
- The painting showing the most hate _____
- The painting with the most flowers _____
- The painting with the most blood _____
- The painting with the most snow _____
- The painting that made you feel insignificant _____
- The painting that made you feel guilty _____
- The painting that made you feel majestic _____
- The painting that made you feel cold _____
- The painting that struck you as warm _____
- The most confusing painting _____
- The most annoying painting _____
- The painting that brought you the most joy _____

The Writing Process—A Summary for Students

A. Pre-writing: Think About It!

   ❑ Brainstorm.
   ❑ Discuss with others.
   ❑ Gather information.
   ❑ Read.
   ❑ Think about what you want to say.
   ❑ Plan how you will say it.

B. Drafting: Write It Down!

   ❑ Organize your thoughts.
   ❑ Choose main ideas.
   ❑ Develop the ideas.
   ❑ Sequence what you want to say.
   ❑ Have others read it and make suggestions.

C. Revising: Make It Better!

   ❑ Read what you have written.
   ❑ Think about what others are saying about your writing.
   ❑ Rearrange—take out and add material.
   ❑ Change words and ideas.
   ❑ Replace often-used words.

D. Editing: Make It Correct!

   ❑ Make sure all sentences are complete.
   ❑ Check grammar, spelling, capitalization, and punctuation.
   ❑ Have someone check your work.
   ❑ Rewrite neatly or print out on the computer.

E. Publishing: Share Your Work with Others!

   ❑ Read aloud your work to a person or a group.
   ❑ Bind your writing in a book.
   ❑ Illustrate your work.
   ❑ Perform your work.
   ❑ Put it to music or combine with dance.

Template for an Integrated Unit

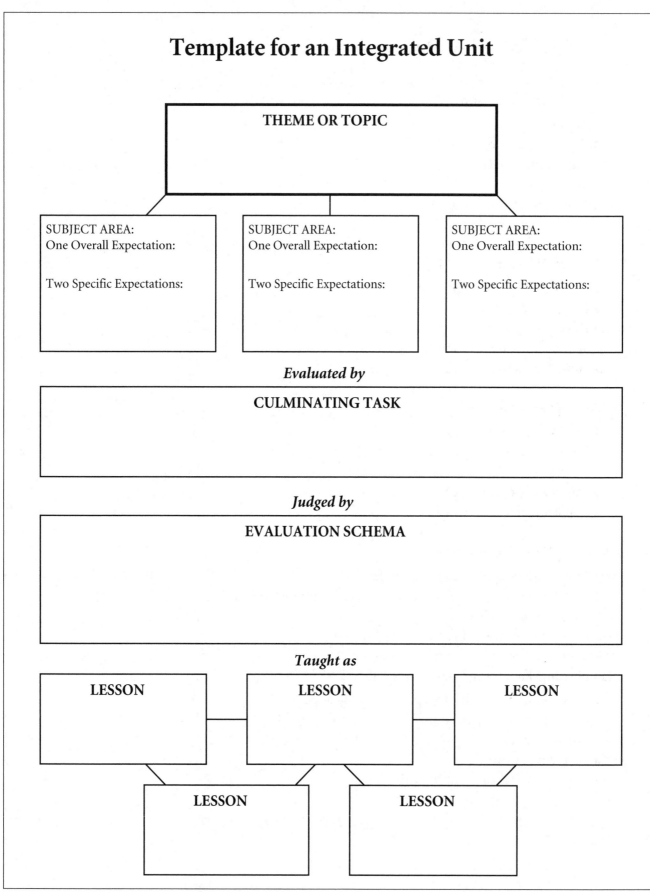

THEME OR TOPIC

SUBJECT AREA:
One Overall Expectation:

Two Specific Expectations:

SUBJECT AREA:
One Overall Expectation:

Two Specific Expectations:

SUBJECT AREA:
One Overall Expectation:

Two Specific Expectations:

Evaluated by

CULMINATING TASK

Judged by

EVALUATION SCHEMA

Taught as

LESSON

LESSON

LESSON

LESSON

LESSON

Recommended Resources

Since many good editions, both softcover and hardcover, exist, only the authors and titles of personally recommended picture books, poetry books, and novels are identified here.

Picture Books

Avi. *Crispin: The Cross of Lead.*
Campbell, Ann-Jeanette. *Dora's Box.*
Choi, Yangsook. *The Name Jar.*
Edwards, Pamela Duncan. *Barefoot: Escape on the Underground Railroad.*
Fleischman, Paul. *Weslandia.*
Fox, Mem. *Whoever You Are.*
Gonsalves, Rob. *Imagine a Night.*
Hest, Amy. *When Jessie Came Across the Sea.*
Hooks, William H. *The Ballad of Belle Dorcas.*
Levine, Karen. *Hana's Suitcase: A True Story.*
Manson, Ainslie, and Karen Reczuch. *Just Like New.*
Martin, Jr., Bill, and John Archambault. *Knots on a Counting Rope.*
Martinez, Alejandro Cruz. *The Woman Who Outshone the Sun: The Legend of Lucia Zenteno.*
McCully, Emily Arnold. *Mirette on the High Wire.*
McDonough, Yona Zeldis. *Peaceful Protest: The Life of Nelson Mandela.*
Mollel, Tololwa M. *The Orphan Boy.*
Mora, Pat. *Tomas and the Library Lady.*
Polacco, Patricia. *Applemando's Dream.*
Raczka, Bob. *No One Saw: Ordinary Things Through the Eyes of an Artist.*
Ringold, Faith. *The Invisible Princess.*
Rose, Deborah Lee. *The People Who Hugged the Trees.*
Van Allsburg, Chris. *The Mysteries of Harris Burdick.*
_____. *The Wretched Stone.*
_____. *The Stranger.*
Van Camp, Richard. *What's the Most Beautiful Thing You Know About Horses?*
Watts, Irene W. *The Fish Princess.*

Wiesner, David. *Tuesday.*
Yee, Paul. *Ghost Train.*
_____. *Roses Sing on New Snow.*
_____. *Tales from Gold Mountain: Stories of the Chinese in the New World.*
Yolen, Jane. *Encounter.*

Poetry

Booth, David, ed. *Images of Nature: Canadian Poets and the Group of Seven.*
Dunn, Sonja. *All Together Now: 200 of Sonja Dunn's Best Chants.*
Fleischman, Paul. *Joyful Noise: Poems for Two Voices.*
Franco, Betsy, ed. *Things I Have to Tell You: Poems and Writing by Teenage Girls.*
Little, Jean. *Hey World, Here I Am.*
Lynne, Sandford. *Ten-Second Rainshowers: Poems by Young People.*
Marsden, John. *Prayer for the Twenty-first Century.*
Morton, Andrew, ed. *101 Poems Against War.*
Nye, Naomi Shihab. *Come with Me: Poems for a Journey.*
_____, ed. *Salting the Ocean: 100 Poems by Young Poets.*
_____. *The Flag of Childhood: Poems from the Middle East.*
Prelutsky, Jack. *Imagine That! Poems of Never-Was.*
Weatherford, Carole Boston. *Remember the Bridge: Poems of a People.*

Novels

Avi. *The True Confessions of Charlotte Doyle.*
Babbitt, Natalie. *Tuck Everlasting.*
Brooks, Martha. *Bone Dance.*
Creech, Sharon. *Walk Two Moons.*
Cushman, Karen. *The Midwife's Apprentice.*
Holman, Felice. *Slake's Limbo.*
Hughes, Ted. *The Iron Man.*
Jocelyn, Marthe. *Earthly Astonishments.*
Konigsburg, E.L. *Silent to the Bone.*
Locker, Thomas. *Sky Tree: Seeing Science Through Art.*
Lowry, Lois. *Gathering Blue.*
_____. *The Giver.*
_____. *Number the Stars.*
MacLachlan, Patricia. *Baby.*
_____. *Sarah, Plain and Tall.*
Matas, Carol. *Jesper.*
_____. *Lisa.*
Newman, Lesléa. *Fat Chance.*
Paterson, Katherine. *The Great Gilly Hopkins.*
_____. *Bridge to Terabithia.*
Spinelli, Jerry. *Wringer.*
_____. *Maniac Magee.*

Professional Reading

Aker, Don. 1995. *Hitting the Mark: Assessment Tools for Teachers*. Markham, ON: Pembroke.

Allen, Janet. 2000. *Yellow Brick Roads: Shared and Guided Paths to Independent Reading, 4–12*. Portland, ME: Stenhouse.

Ayers, W., and T. Miller, eds. 1998. *A Light in Dark Times: Maxine Greene and the Unfinished Conversation*. New York: Teachers College Press.

Barton, Bob. 2000. *Telling Stories Your Way: Storytelling and Reading Aloud in the Classroom*. Markham, ON: Pembroke.

Booth, David. 2002. *Even Hockey Players Read: Boys, Literacy and Learning*. Markham, ON: Pembroke.

————, ed. 1996. *Literacy Techniques for Building Successful Readers and Writers*. Markham, ON: Pembroke.

————. 1986. *Story Drama: Reading, Writing and Role-playing Across the Curriculum*. Markham, ON: Pembroke.

Booth, David, and Jonothan Neelands, eds. 1998. *Writing in Role: Classroom Projects Connecting Writing and Drama*. Hamilton, ON: Caliburn Enterprises.

Booth, David, Jack Booth, and Jo Phenix. 1994. *Assessment and Evaluation Techniques and Strategies for Use with Children Ages 5–9*. Toronto: Harcourt Brace.

Booth, David, and Charles J. Lundy. 1985. *Improvisation: Learning Through Drama*. Toronto: Harcourt Brace Jovanovich.

Calkins, Lucy McCormick, and Shelley Harwayne. 1991. *Living Between the Lines*. Portsmouth, NH: Heinemann.

Cambourne, Brian. 1988. *The Whole Story: Natural Learning and the Acquisition of Literacy in the Classroom*. Auckland, AU: Ashton Scholastic.

Christensen, Linda. 2000. *Reading, Writing, and Rising Up: Teaching About Social Justice and the Power of the Written Word*. Milwaukee, WI: Rethinking Schools.

Duquette, Cheryl. 2001. *Students at Risk: Solutions to Classroom Challenges*. Markham, ON: Pembroke.

Eisner, Elliot, ed. 1976. *The Arts, Human Development and Education*. Berkeley, CA: McCutchan Publishers.

Franklin, Ursula. 1990. *The Real World of Technology.* Massey Lectures Series. Toronto: House of Anansi Press.

Freire, Paulo. 2001. *Pedagogy of Freedom: Ethics, Democracy and Civic Courage.* New York: Rowman and Littlefield.

Frost, Helen. 2001. *When I Whisper, Nobody Listens: Helping Young People Write About Difficult Issues.* Portsmouth, NH: Heinemann.

Gallagher, Kathleen. 2000. *Drama Education in the Lives of Girls.* Toronto: University of Toronto Press.

Gardner, Howard. 1983. *Frames of Mind: The Theory of Multiple Intelligences.* New York: Basic Books.

Giroux, Henry. 1981. "Toward a New Sociology of Curriculum." In *Curriculum and Instruction: Alternatives in Education,* edited by H. Giroux, A. Penna, and W. Pinar, pp. 98–108. Berkeley, CA: McCutchan Publishing.

Goleman, Daniel. 1995. *Emotional Intelligence.* New York: Bantam Books.

Greene, Maxine. 2001. *Variations on a Blue Guitar: The Lincoln Center Institute Lectures on Aesthetic Education.* New York: Teachers College Press.

_____. 1995. *Releasing the Imagination: Essay on Education, the Arts, and Social Change.* San Francisco: Jossey-Bass.

hooks, bell. 1994. *Teaching to Transgress: Education as the Practice of Freedom.* New York: Routledge.

Johnson, David W., and Frank P. Johnson. 1991. *Joining Together: Group Theory and Group Skills.* Needham Heights, MA: Allyn and Bacon.

Koechlin, Carol, and Sandi Zwaan. 2001. *Info Tasks for Successful Learning: Building Skills in Reading, Writing and Research.* Markham, ON: Pembroke.

Kohl, Herbert R. 1998. *The Discipline of Hope: Learning from a Lifetime of Teaching.* New York: Simon & Schuster.

_____. 1994. *I Won't Learn from You: And Other Thoughts on Creative Maladjustment.* New York: The New Press.

Little, Jean. 1990. *Stars Come Out Within.* Markham, ON: Viking/Penguin Books.

Lundy, Charles, and David Booth. 1985. *Interpretation: Working with Scripts.* Toronto: Harcourt Brace Jovanovich.

Lundy, Kathleen Gould, Christine Jackson, Lorna Wilson, and Lorraine Sutherns. 2001. *The Treasure Chest: Story, Drama and Dance/Movement in the Classroom.* Toronto: Toronto District School Board.

McIntosh, Peggy, and Emily Style. 1999. "Curriculum as Window and Mirror." The SEED Project on Inclusive Curriculum (Seeking Educational Equity and Diversity). Wellesley College Center for Research on Women.

Moffett, James, and Betty Jane Wagner. 1992. *Student-centered Language Arts, K–12.* Portsmouth, NH: Heinemann/Boyton Cook.

Morgan, Norah, and Juliana Saxton. 1994. *Asking Better Questions.* Markham, ON: Pembroke.

Neelands, Jonothan. 1992. *Structuring Drama Work.* Cambridge: Cambridge University Press.

_____. 1984. *Making Sense of Drama: A Guide to Classroom Practice.* London: Heinemann.

Paterson, Katherine. 1989. *The Spying Heart: More Thoughts on Reading and Writing Books for Children.* New York: E.P. Dutton.

_____. 1988. *Gates of Excellence: On Reading and Writing Books for Children.* New York: E.P. Dutton.

Pennac, Daniel. 1994. *Better Than Life: The Secrets of Reading.* Markham, ON: Pembroke; Portland, ME: Stenhouse.

Pepler, D.J., W.M. Craig, S. Ziegler, and A. Charach. 1994. "An Evaluation of an Anti-bullying Intervention in Toronto Schools." *Canadian Journal of Community Mental Health* 13: 95–100.

Phenix, Jo. 2002. *The Writing Teacher's Handbook.* Markham, ON: Pembroke.

Rigby, Ken. 2001. *Stop the Bullying: A Handbook for Teachers.* Markham, ON: Pembroke.

_____. 1998. *Bullying in Schools and What to Do About It.* Markham, ON: Pembroke.

Rosen, Michael. 1989. *Did I Hear You Write?* Richmond Hill, ON: Scholastic.

Schniedewind, Nancy, and Ellen Davidson. 1998. *Open Minds to Equality: A Source Book of Learning Activities to Affirm Diversity and Promote Equity.* Boston: Allyn and Bacon.

Schwartz, Susan, and Mindy Pollishuke. 2002. *Creating the Dynamic Classroom: A Handbook for Teachers.* Toronto: Irwin.

Swartz, Larry. 2002. *The New Dramathemes.* Markham, ON: Pembroke.

Swartz, Larry, and David Booth. 1996. *Novel Sense.* Toronto: Harcourt Brace.

Tierney, Robert J., Mark A. Carter, and Laura E. Desai. 1991. *Portfolio Assessment in the Reading-Writing Classroom.* Norwood, MA: Christopher Gordon Publishers.

Tovani, Cris. 2004. *Do I Really Have to Teach Reading? Content Comprehension, Grades 6–12.* Portland, ME: Stenhouse.

_____. 2000. *I Read It But I Don't Get It: Comprehension Strategies for Adolescent Learners.* Portland, ME: Stenhouse.

Worthy, Jo, and Kathryn Prater. 2002. "'I Thought About It All Night': Readers Theatre for Reading Fluency and Motivation." *The Reading Teacher* 56(3): 296.

Index

Allen, Janet, 32
anecdotal records, 75–76
Arthur series, 62
artifacts, using, 30–32, 91, 92
Applause Connection game, 40
Asking Better Questions, 58
assessment, nature of, 74–75, 79–80
assessment checklist, 91, 92, 93

Barefoot, 27
bird's eye view, 53, 68
Bontemps, Arna, 45
Booth, David, 62, 72
brainstorming, 36–37
Bridges, Ruby, 39
bullying, 40–41

Calkins, Lucy McCormick, 91
Cambourne, Brian, 13
character study, 66–67
"Choice, The," 33
choral speaking, 48–49, 52
Christensen, Linda, 25
choreography. *See* movement.
classroom as community, 5, 8, 10,
    11–13, 28
cooperative games, 19, 20, 21, 22,
    23, 40, 41
corridor of voices, 61
Courtney, Richard, 87
culminating task, 30, 87–94
curriculum, 8, 29, 43–56, 87
Cushman, Karen, 54
"cut to…" strategy, 44–46, 71

Discipline of Hope, The, 7
diversity, 10, 13
Dora's Box, 31, 32

Einstein, Albert, 75
Eisner, Elliot, 29
Encounter, 65, 68
engaging the students, 29–42

English as a second language, 64
establishing the learning
    environment, 11–28
evaluating and assessing the
    learning, 74–95
evaluation, personal and group, 94
exemplars, 79
Experts Tell Us game, 41–42, 52
exploring the curriculum, 43–56
extending the learning, 57–73

Fat Chance, 32
field trips, 63–64
Freire, Paulo, 56, 58
Fuentes, Glenys McQueen, 64, 65,
    66

Gallagher, Kathleen, 37, 58
Gardner, Howard, 13
Ginatt, Haim, 12
Giroux, Henry, 24
Giver, The, 46, 68–70
goals and needs, sharing, 16–17, 18,
    77
graphic organizers, 49–50
Greene, Maxine, 43, 57
greeting and checking in, 13–14
group work, 34, 40, 66, 74, 89,
    91–94
guiding metaphors for classrooms,
    8–9

Hana's Suitcase, 67
Hatchet, 32
Heathcoate, Dorothy, 39
hieroglyphics strategy, 64–66
historical documents, 63
Holman, Felice, 67
Home children, 91, 92, 93
hooks, bell, 11, 28
"hooks," 29, 30, 31
Hughes, Ted, 67

"I am from…" strategy, 25–27, 91
Inner/Outer Circle, 60, 70
integrated unit, 87, 89, 90
interviewing, 17–19, 41–42, 76–78
In the Freedom of Dreams, 22, 51
Invisible Princess, The, 24, 46
Iron Man, The, 62
I see, I wonder, I hope writing, 5–7,
    53

journals, 63, 75, 80–81

kids, questions about, 17, 25, 33, 34,
    39, 40, 48, 49, 53, 55, 59, 61, 64,
    67, 71, 77, 80, 89
Kohl, Herbert, 7
Konigsburg, E.L., 34

language registers, 39, 52
link between learning & students'
    lives, 30, 56
list making, 31, 33–34
Login centre, 14–15, 77
looking at pictures, 34, 35, 63, 64
Lowry, Lois, 46, 68
Lundell, Margo, 39

Mandela, Nelson, 22, 52
Marsden, John, 60
Mattawa, Khaled, 49
McIntosh, Peggy, 8–9
Midwife's Apprentice, The, 54, 68
Miller, Michael, 22, 51
minimal scripts, 50–51
Moffett, James, 47, 87
Mollel, Tololwa M., 25
monologue, 50, 52
Morgan, Norah, 58
movement, 55–56, 65–66
multiple intelligences, 89
Munch, Edvard, 34
museum as culminating task, 91–93
"My Heart Is in My Throat," 9–10

Mysteries of Harris Burdick, The, 34

name games, 19–21
Neelands, Jonothan, 50
"Night in Al-Hamra," 49

o'huigin, sean, 39
Open Minds to Equality, 28
Orphan Boy, The, 25, 27

Paterson, Katherine, 30, 49
Peplar, Debra, 41
personal stories, 24–25
picture books, 24, 25, 50, 55
poetry sources, 46, 49, 91
portfolios, 83–84, 85–86
Prater, Kathryn, 62
Prayer for the 21st Century, 24, 60
prior knowledge, 30
prompts to reflection, 16, 26, 76, 77, 78
Purdy, Al, 39

questioning strategies, 58
Questions to Ask Yourself, 13, 30, 44, 58, 75
quotations, working with, 22, 24, 53–54

Readers Theatre, 52, 61–63, 93
reading aloud, 32–33
Real World of Technology, The, 7
"Remember the Bridge," 59
Reynolds, Howard, 39
Riel, Louis, 27, 31, 67
Ringold, Faith, 24, 46
role. *See* student in role; teacher in role.

role on the wall, 42, 50, 55–56
Roosevelt, Eleanor, 22
Rosen, Michael, 59
rubric, 72, 79, 82–83

Saxton, Juliana, 58
scaffolding, 11–12
Schecter, Richard, 52
"Scream, The," 34
seeing in different ways, 63–64
Seeking Educational Equity and Diversity Project, 8
Shakespeare, William, 54
Silent to the Bone, 32, 34, 41–42, 60–61, 68
Slake's Limbo, 67
soundscape, 47, 55, 92
"Southern Mansion," 45, 46, 48
starting lines, 50, 51
Stiggins, Richard, 74
student profiles, 79
students
    feedback to, 12–13
    finding voices, 9–10, 34
    negotiating with, 12
    reproducible pages for, 15, 18, 22, 35, 78, 81, 85–86, 88
    what helps them learn, 43–44
students in role, 39, 41–42, 47, 48, 52, 67–68, 69–70, 91, 92, 93
Style, Emily, 8–9
Swartz, Larry, 72

tableaux, 44, 45, 46, 47, 48, 49, 52, 71, 91
teachable moment, 7
teacher, roles played by, 57–58
teacher in role, 38–39, 52, 71, 91

teaching "hard" skills in soft ways, 7–8
Through My Eyes, 39
thumbnail sketches, 50
Tierney, Robert J., 83
True Confessions of Charlotte Doyle, The, 32
Tuck Everlasting, 61
Tutu, Desmond, 21

Van Allsburg, Chris, 34, 71
Van Camp, Richard, 37
Vygotsky, Lev, 11, 12, 14

Wagner, Betty, 87
Walk Around Reading, 39–40, 48
Walk of Words, 22, 24
"We are from…" activity, 26–27
Weatherford, Carole Boston, 49
What's the Most Beautiful Thing You Know About Horses?, 37
When Jessie Came Across the Sea, 50
Woman Who Outshone the Sun, The, 50, 55–56, 67
word discoveries, 53–54
Worthy, Jo, 62
Wretched Stone, The, 68, 71–72
Wringer, 27, 32, 50, 53, 68
writing, 25–27, 53, 59–60, 61, 67–70, 71–72, 80, 81

Yellow Brick Roads, 32
Yolen, Jane, 65
Young, Wayland, 33
Youssef, Saadi, 49

Acknowledgments

Every effort has been made to contact copyright holders for permission to reproduce borrowed material. The publishers apologize for any such omissions and will be pleased to rectify them in subsequent reprints of the book.

"The Bud" excerpt from "Saint Francis and the Sow" by Galway Kinnell, in *Mortal Acts, Mortal Words* (Boston: Houghton Mifflin,1980).

"My Heart Is in My Throat" by Erin B. Henry, in *Things I Have to Tell You: Poems and Writing by Teenage Girls*, edited by Betsy Franco (New York: Candlewick Press, 2003).

"Night in Al-Hamra" by Saadi Youssef and translated by Khaled Mattawa, in *101 Poems Against War*, edited by Andrew Morton (New York: Faber and Faber, 2003).

"Southern Mansion" by Arna Bontemps, found at www.americanpoems.com, a Web site constructed by Gunnar Bengtsson.

"We Are From…" collective poem by York University, Faculty of Education students, in the ED 1 Common Year course 2000, 02–03, in the Concurrent Program; course directed by Marcela Duran.

The "woman" monologue by Michael Miller, from *In the Freedom of Dreams*, produced at the Lorraine Kimsa Theatre for Young People in Toronto in 2003.

Many thanks to the teachers, social workers, psychologists, and students in the Toronto, York Region, and Durham Catholic District School Boards for inviting me into their schools over the years and for allowing me to be both a guest teacher and a learner. Thanks too to the Fine Arts teacher candidates at York University, Faculty of Education (02–03 and 03–04) for "honest talk" and generous feedback about the process of learning how to teach Junior and Intermediate students.